SHARPENING

SHARPENING

A WOODWORKER'S GUIDE

RANDALL A. MAXEY

GUILD OF MASTER CRAFTSMAN PUBLICATIONS LTD

CONTENTS

Introduction

A sharp tool is a joy to use. A kitchen knife that cuts cleanly and effortlessly makes time in the kitchen more enjoyable. Garden tools with a keen edge make digging and weeding easier. For the do-it-yourselfer and woodworker, sharp chisels, hand planes and carving tools slice cleanly through wood fibres for the ultimate surface finish.

For most of us, however, the thought of sharpening the tools we use can be intimidating. What products do I need to get the sharpest edge? What techniques yield the best results? How do I know if the edge is truly sharp? In short, we're afraid that we'll somehow ruin the tool if we attempt to sharpen it.

The good news is that anyone can learn to sharpen. The goal of this book is to explain what sharpness really is and to show you some easy tools and techniques you can use to get the sharpest edge. You'll learn about different sharpening methods so that you can find the one that works for you and your budget. You'll get all the basic information you need that guarantees success.

Stay sharp!
Randy Maxey

1
Getting started

1:1

Understanding sharpness

The purpose of this book is to show you just how easy it is to learn to sharpen tools, knives and other items that have a cutting edge.

In basic terms, sharpening boils down to using an abrasive to remove steel to obtain a sharp edge. But before we start talking about the 'how' of sharpening, we first need to discuss the definition of sharpness.

We'll discuss what it means for a tool to be really sharp and why dull tools create problems when we try to use them. It all goes back to secondary school geometry. You don't need a mathematics degree to understand what makes a tool's edge razor sharp. Understanding the fundamentals will get you on the road to sharpening success.

An abrasive sharpening medium, like a waterstone, helps form a razor-sharp edge on knives and other tools.

Sharpness and dullness

I'm sure you've had the experience of picking up a knife or chisel to use it and then discovering that it doesn't really cut as it should. In short, the tool is dull. But what does this mean?

To understand the difference between sharpness and dullness, we must think a little about geometry. If you draw two intersecting straight lines on paper, the intersection of those two lines is a point.

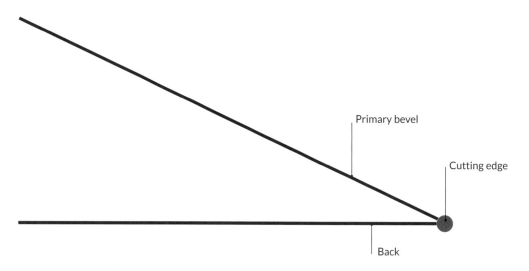

ABOVE *The intersection of two lines is a single point in space.*

Now, if you convert those lines into flat planes, the intersection of the two planes becomes a straight line. This concept is fundamental to understanding what sharpness really means.

Taking this illustration a little further, if you look at the cutting edge of a knife or chisel, for example, the flat surfaces that form the cutting edge should, in theory, form a line of sharpness.

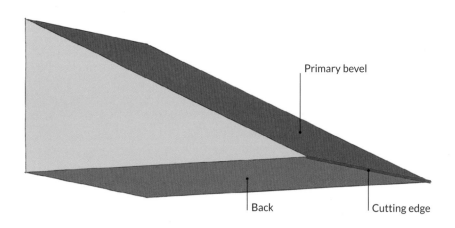

ABOVE *A straight line is formed at the intersection of two planes.*

What makes a tool dull?

Over time, with use, that sharp edge wears down and becomes more rounded. It's a fact of life and expected during the lifetime of a tool. How fast that edge becomes dull is determined by several factors including the material it's cutting, the type of steel in the blade and how the tool is being used.

BELOW *A cutting edge becomes dull as it wears down and forms more of a rounded edge.*

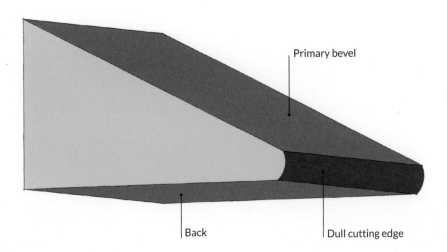

Primary bevel

Back

Dull cutting edge

Dull is dangerous

You may have heard it said that a dull tool is more dangerous than a sharp tool. One reason for this is that a dull tool is more likely to slip instead of engaging, or cutting into, the object you're cutting. The rounded edge can't 'grab' and make a clean cut. Think of trying to cut a tomato with a knife. With a nice, sharp edge, the knife blade will cut through the skin of the tomato with almost no pressure at all. If the edge is dull, the knife is more likely to crush the tomato before it starts cutting. Sometimes the knife blade will slip across the surface of the tomato instead of slicing.

Therefore, a dull pocketknife is a particular concern. Many times, a pocketknife is used to cut an object held in your opposite hand. If the edge is dull, you'll naturally put more pressure on the knife to try to get it to cut. The dull edge can cause the blade to slip and cut the soft tissue of your hand or fingers instead.

Conversely, a sharp knife will 'bite' into the object you're cutting and should require little effort to make the cut. Using a sharp tool is always more predictable and safer than using a dull one. This point will be driven home as you gain more experience with sharpening.

1:2
Bevel angles

We've already seen that sharpness is defined by the intersection of two planes. The angle at which these two planes intersect is called the bevel angle. Some tools, such as chisels and hand plane irons, have a single bevel. In other words, the bevel is only formed on one side of the blade. The back of the blade forms one plane. The bevel forms the other plane that intersects with the back plane to form the cutting edge. You'll learn the importance of keeping these two intersecting surfaces flat and polished.

Knives usually feature a double bevel with a bevel ground on each side of the steel. In this case, the actual bevel angle is relative to the centre line of the blade. Where these two bevels of a knife edge intersect forms the cutting edge.

A bevelled cutting edge on a tool forms the foundation for keeping the tool sharp for optimum performance.

Bevel angles and function

The angle of the bevel is determined by the intended function of the tool. Knives typically have more acute angles that create the cutting edge. The thin steel of the knife ground with a double bevel creates a razor-sharp edge ideal for slicing. Items made for chopping, like cleavers and axes, are usually made with thicker steel and less acute bevels. This creates a stronger cutting edge more suitable for the impact of chopping that might otherwise damage the edge of a thinner knife.

The same philosophy or design intent holds true with woodworking tools. Some types of chisels are designed to be struck with a mallet to chop and remove waste from a workpiece. These will have strong edges with less acute bevels. Paring chisels, by contrast, are designed to be used with hand pressure only and excel at severing wood fibres in thin slices. The lower bevel angle creates more of a knife edge that makes this task easier than with traditional bench chisels.

Double bevel

Single bevel

Single bevel and double bevel. Some tools like chisels and plane irons feature a single bevel. Knives are usually ground with a double bevel.

Blade back

When I teach folks how to sharpen tools like plane irons and chisels, most assume that sharpening means addressing the bevel of the blade. But that's only part of the solution to getting a keen cutting edge. Remember that sharpness is defined by the intersection of two *flat* planes.

For single-bevel tools, it's not only the flatness of the bevel that matters. The back of the blade also plays a key role in the sharpness of the cutting edge. If the bevel or the back of the blade isn't truly flat, it's difficult – if not impossible – to obtain a sharp, straight edge. On double-bevel tools like knives, there is no 'back' of the blade as it pertains to the cutting edge. It's all about the bevels.

In Section 2:1, I'll guide you through the process of flattening the back of a chisel. In Section 2:2, you'll use the same method for flattening the back of an iron (blade) for a hand plane.

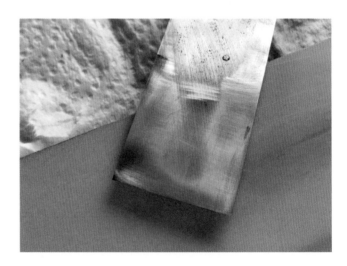

On single-bevel tools like this chisel, if the blade is twisted or the back exhibits a crowned or convex area, sharpening will be difficult until the back is flattened near the cutting edge.

Primary bevel

For single-bevel tools, once you have the back of a blade flat, it's time to concentrate on the bevel. For double-bevel tools, sharpness is all about the line formed at the apex of the two bevels.

Sharpening a bevel gets us towards the goal of sharpness. In theory, our goal is to form an infinitely thin line at the cutting edge.

As you'll learn in Section 1:4, there is a wide variety of abrasive products and tools that you can use to sharpen tools.

As you gain experience with sharpening and honing, you'll soon recognize what 'sharp' really means and when a tool needs to be touched up.

Sharpening is all about keeping the cutting edge as thin and straight as possible.

The back and bevel of this chisel have been flattened and the bevel honed to a sharp edge.

Sharpening vs. honing

Sometimes you'll hear two terms that are often used interchangeably: sharpening and honing. But they don't really mean the same thing.

For the purposes of this book, I consider sharpening the initial process of shaping and refining the cutting edge. Honing is a secondary step where the edge is polished to a razor-sharp edge. Barbers will often use a leather strop that is charged with a fine polishing compound to hone their razors.

As you use a tool, you'll start to feel when it's not cutting as well as it initially did. Touching up the edge by honing with a fine abrasive is often all you'll need to do. It's quick and easy and lets you get right back to work. If the cutting edge is somehow damaged, you'll need to go back and sharpen it and go through the honing process once again.

1:3
Types of steel

No discussion of sharpening is complete without at least a mention of steel types. Tool and knife manufacturers have spent decades and, in some cases, centuries refining the ingredients and process of making steel. Worldwide, there are over 3,500 different types of steel. Fortunately, there are only a few general types that apply to the tools and accessories shown in this book.

In this section I will discuss the most common types of steel you are likely to come across. This is not meant to be a scientific, metallurgical dissertation but a brief overview as it pertains to sharpening.

Steel is smelted in a furnace and rolled into sheets for further processing into tool components such as knives, chisels and plane irons.

How steel is made

First, let's consider how the steel in edge tools is made. Regardless of the chemical composition, iron and other additives are smelted in a high-temperature furnace. While the mixture is pourable, it can be forged, poured in a casting or rolled into sheets or other shapes. Sometimes it can be cast into billets that can later be cold-rolled into sheets.

Metals used for tools and knives are further processed by the manufacturer or toolmaker. Once a blade is cut and formed into a rough version of its final shape and size, it goes through a heat-treatment process to harden the steel. The steel is heated to a high temperature, then quickly dipped in oil or water to quench it. This hardens the steel but results in a rather brittle steel. A secondary tempering process slightly heats the steel, which is then cooled slowly to create a steel that is less brittle and of suitable hardness and toughness for its intended use.

Types of steel

When you shop for tools, you may run across an alphabet soup of labels for the steel such as Cr-V, O1, A2 and others. These are simply referencing the type of steel the blade is made from. Below I discuss the most common types of steel you're likely to encounter in tools.

Chrome-Vanadium
Walk through any store that sells mechanics' tools such as spanners and you are likely to see 'Cr-V' or 'Chrome-Vanadium' proudly stamped on the product. Cr-V steel resists corrosion well and is typically harder than other common steels used in cutting tools. Those properties make it a great choice for tools such as spanners and pliers. Depending on the amount of vanadium in the steel, Cr-V steel is not a great choice for tools that require a keen cutting edge. Because of its large carbide particles it can be difficult to sharpen and maintain an edge on a blade made from Cr-V steel.

Tools used by mechanics are often made from Chrome-Vanadium steel.

O1

Steels made with a higher carbon content are more suitable for knife blades and woodworking tools given their ability to hold an edge once they are sharpened. One of the most popular types of high-carbon steel is labelled 'O1', meaning it has been quenched with oil during the heat-treatment process. It results in a tough steel that is easy to sharpen to a fine edge and holds the edge well.

When the edge begins to dull, it is a quick task to hone the edge and get back to work.

I have a very old pocketknife with blades made from high-carbon steel. The blades have dark stains on them and perhaps some light rust, but I can keep the cutting edge impressively sharp.

O1 steel can be sharpened with any sharpening abrasive including waterstones, diamond stones and ceramic stones.

A hand plane using an O1 steel iron can easily be sharpened to a keen edge.

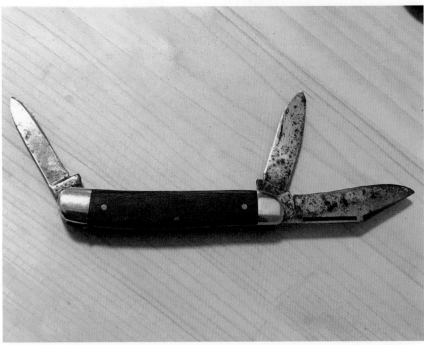

This old pocketknife has high-carbon steel blades that can still hold a sharp edge despite the discolouration and stains in the steel.

A2

Another popular steel, especially among woodworkers, is A2 tool steel. As the letter 'A' implies, it is air-hardened instead of being quenched in water or oil. This results in a tough steel that can hold an edge longer than O1 steel. Cryogenic treatment, or subjecting the steel to temperatures of −320°F (−195°C) in a freezer, creates small carbide particles in the steel that are very tough. A2 steel is tougher and longer-wearing at the cutting edge than O1 steel.

It should be noted that A2 steel can never be sharpened to as fine an edge as O1 steel due to a larger particle size in the steel structure. 'Sharpness' is a relative term, however, and for a lot of woodworkers, the ability to retain an edge longer than O1 steel offsets this minor shortcoming. If you work with a lot of exotic wood species that contain large amounts of silica, A2 tool steel for chisels and planes would be a great option. Sharpening A2 steel requires a little more effort than O1 steel and will tend to wear down conventional abrasives faster. Although you can use higher-quality waterstones, diamond stones might be a better, more durable, option if you sharpen A2 steel frequently.

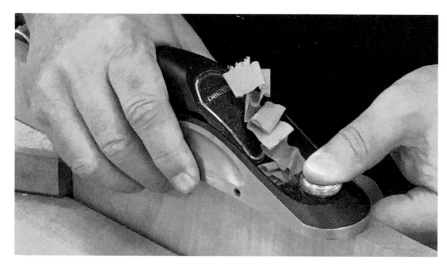

While A2 steel may not get as sharp as O1 steel on a microscopic level, it can still be honed to a razor edge sharp enough to slice through end-grain wood fibres.

A2 steel holds an edge that is a little more durable than O1 steel and is found in many plane irons and chisels.

High-speed steel

High-speed steel (HS or HSS) was originally formulated to retain a cutting edge for applications where the tool would be subject to high heat such as drilling or machining metal. Its advantages are high hardness and high abrasion resistance while being able to maintain an edge. Sometimes you will see the label for the specific type of steel such as 'M1', 'M2', 'M7' and so on. You'll find that most drill bits are made from high-speed steel. The addition of cobalt creates higher heat resistance.

Other than drill bits, a common use for HSS in woodworking is in tools used for turning wood on a lathe. When turning wood, friction causes the cutting edge to heat up. If this were a common carbon-steel tool, this high heat would be likely to ruin the temper of the steel. HSS tools, however, can take the heat without compromising the cutting edge.

If you're trying to sharpen high-speed steel, it is best to use diamond sharpeners or special cubic boron nitride (CBN) grinding wheels.

Cr-Mn

Chrome-manganese steel is another high-carbon alloy, but it goes through a different heat-treatment process. Instead of being heated, quickly quenched in water or oil, then tempered, Cr-Mn steel goes through a special, slower isothermal hardening method.

The steel is quenched in a bath of molten salt at 390°F (200°C), left to soak until the steel's desired crystalline structure is fully formed, and then cooled to room temperature in a water shower. This highly controlled process results in a steel with a fine, uniform grain structure that enables it to take and hold an edge very well.

Cr-Mn steel doesn't contain enough chromium to prevent rusting, so a wipe down with a light oil or wax will help keep the tool rust-free, particularly in humid environments.

As for sharpening Cr-Mn steel, you can use the same abrasives and tools you would use on any high-carbon steel. You'll find that sharpening and honing Cr-Mn steel results in a long-lasting sharp edge.

This chisel blade is made from chrome-manganese steel. The special heat-treatment process results in a tough, durable steel that holds an edge well.

Powdered Metal Steel

The use of powdered metal alloys in woodworking tools is a recent innovation. It is made differently than traditional steel. The steel has a higher vanadium content. Vanadium carbide particles have the advantage of being very small and quite durable. High-vanadium molten steel is sprayed into a vacuum chamber where the particles cool. This resulting powder is compressed and sintered under high heat and pressure until it can be rolled into sheets. This high-vanadium steel has a much lower particle size than other steels, which makes it an attractive option for knifemakers and toolmakers since it can be sharpened to a fine, durable edge.

Powdered-metal cutting tools aren't as common as high-carbon steel tools, but one woodworking tool manufacturer, Lee Valley Tools, offers it as an option for their hand planes and chisels, using a proprietary powdered metal labelled 'PM-V11' on their Veritas-branded tools.

This plane features an iron made from powdered metal. Its sharpened edge is longer-lasting than some other steels.

The cost of PM-V11 steel is only marginally higher than O1 steel, but offers some distinct advantages. As mentioned earlier, it can be sharpened to a razor-sharp edge because of the smaller particle size in the steel matrix. The steel is more durable than O1 or A2 steels. PM-V11 is only slightly harder to sharpen than O1, but once sharp it will hold an edge longer.

You can use any conventional abrasive media to sharpen PM-V11, but I recommend using high-quality waterstones or diamond stones.

Powdered metal plane irons can be sharpened with conventional sharpening abrasives to attain a razor-sharp edge.

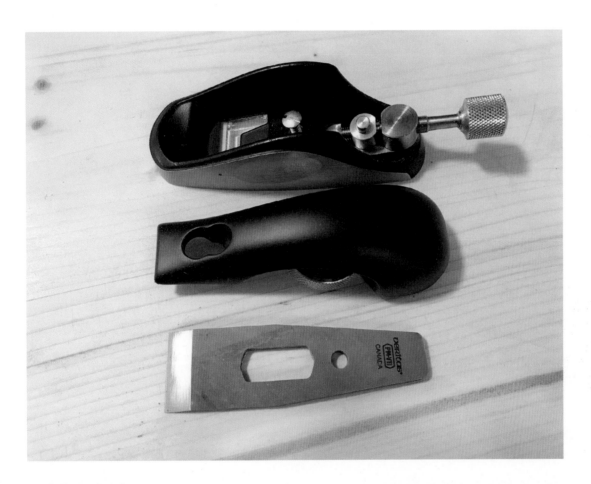

Stainless steel

To resist rust and corrosion, steel manufacturers add chromium and nickel to create what we know as stainless steel. Although stainless steel is great for some applications where the steel is subject to wet or corrosive environments, it's not that great for holding an edge on tools and knives. Some knife manufacturers try to improve this characteristic by adding higher levels of carbon. While this may slightly improve the ability to get the tool sharp, it won't be as sharp or hold an edge as well as high-carbon steels like O1 or A2.

You'll find a lot of inexpensive knives made from stainless steel. The manufacturers want their products to have the best appearance on the store shelf without showing any rust stains. It is possible to sharpen higher-quality stainless steel knives to a keen edge. However, I prefer knives with a higher carbon content that are easier to sharpen to a razor-sharp edge. For woodworking tools, I stay away from stainless steel altogether.

Carbide

Tungsten carbide is a common material used in woodworking tools such as saw blades and router bits. You'll also find it in some knife sharpeners. It is extremely hard and wear-resistant. It can also stand up to the high temperatures encountered when cutting and routing wood.

Carbide is formed in the manner similar to powdered metals mentioned above. Tungsten carbide particles are mixed with binders and wax to form the rough final shape. The parts are sintered, or heated, at very high temperatures in a vacuum to bind all the components together.

Carbide is expensive to manufacture, so it is usually used in small quantities to form cutting edges on saw blades and router bits. Carbide is also difficult to sharpen – diamond abrasive tools are the only real option for sharpening. If you take a close look at the cutting edge on a carbide tool, you'll notice a high cutting angle. This is because carbide is very brittle and the higher angle helps reinforce the cutting edge.

As I mentioned, when it comes to sharpening carbide tools like router bits, diamond stones are your only option (see page 37).

Carbide steel is often found on router bits and saw blades. Carbide forms a tough edge that stays sharp much longer than tool steel.

Japanese tool steel

Many Japanese tools including knives, hand plane irons and chisels follow a tradition of metalworking that dates back centuries. Ancient makers of Samurai swords learned a method of metalworking and forging that some toolmakers still use today.

Metalsmiths forge a laminated steel that starts with a layer of high-carbon steel where the cutting edge will be formed. Softer steel is then laminated with softer iron to reinforce that high-carbon layer and make the blade less brittle. These techniques were developed over hundreds of years and each blade was forged by hand by a master blade-maker.

Today, you can still find tools made by hand by master craftspeople in Japan. You can spend hundreds of pounds on a chisel or hand plane made by a craftsperson with a good reputation. Fortunately, less expensive, mass-produced options are available at a lower cost, but some purists insist on only the best from the most reputable makers.

Sharpening an authentic Japanese-made plane iron is traditionally done with high-quality waterstones. Ceramic waterstones are also a popular option. Some woodworkers believe that a good-quality Japanese steel can be sharpened to an edge sharper than most other steels.

LEFT: *This Japanese hand plane utilizes a laminated steel blade. Traditionally, these were made by highly skilled blacksmiths.*

BELOW: *If you look closely, you can see the laminations in the steel of these Japanese-made chisels and plane iron.*

1:4
Tools and supplies

When you reduce sharpening and honing to the basics, it is about using an abrasive to remove metal. That abrasive can take an endless number of forms and types. Add to that the wide variety of jigs, accessories and machines that claim to make sharpening easier and you're left with a dizzying array of products that can suck money out of your pocket before you know it.

In this section, I'll cover the basic supplies you should consider for your sharpening needs. There are so many products, in fact, that it can be downright confusing trying to choose which ones to purchase and use for sharpening tools and knives. I'll break down the categories of sharpening abrasives and accessories so you can gain familiarity with just a few of them.

This sample of sharpening accessories is only a small fraction of what is available.

Choosing an abrasive

If you are just starting out in your sharpening venture and shopping for products, two guidelines I use are the cost and the longevity of the sharpening abrasive. There is a trade-off: low-cost sharpening media typically do not last as long as higher-priced options. More durable solutions tend to cost more. But if you're starting out, it's okay to start on the low-end of the budget spectrum until you get some practice using proper sharpening methods and techniques. Then you'll be able to upgrade to better equipment as your budget allows.

A word about grit size

Before we start in on our discussion of abrasives, we need to talk about grit sizes. Regardless of which sharpening media you use, you should be familiar with the range of grits available.

When we talk about grit size, we're talking about the average size of the abrasive particles used in the sharpening media. You'll find a variety of materials that are used to create the abrasive particles, but their size is a common denominator among all of them.

The chart below shows how grit sizes compare to micron size. Unfortunately, manufacturers will often use a different system for labelling their grit sizes. Their numbering system may not match those shown in this chart. Some only use the designations 'Coarse', 'Medium', 'Fine' and so on. Where possible, seek out the equivalent micron size; microns are a universally recognized reference for particle size.

Without getting into the various international standards for abrasive particle size, in general terms, the coarser abrasives with larger particle size are designed to remove material quickly. For sharpening purposes, the coarse abrasives are usually reserved for repairing a damaged cutting edge that has been nicked or is extremely dull. These abrasives will

Don't be overwhelmed by the choices in sharpening supplies. Start with a basic set, gain some experience, then expand your supplies as needed.

Micron (1/1000 mm)	Grit size
162	P100
100	P150
68	P220
35	P400
26	P600
22	P800
18	P1000
15	P1200
12	P1500
10	P2000
3	P4000
1.2	P8000

The coarse grit on this waterstone makes quick work of reshaping a cutting edge.

The smaller abrasive particles on this waterstone create a mirror polish for the sharpest edge on your tools.

leave deep scratches in the metal that need to be removed by the finer grits.

Fine-grit abrasives, with their smaller particle size, are designed for final honing and polishing of the cutting edge. Their job is to remove the scratches left by coarser grits. Once a tool is properly sharpened, touching up, or honing, the edge periodically is done with the finer grits.

When sharpening, it is best to have a wide variety of grit sizes at your disposal. One question I hear a lot is, 'How do you know which grit to start with when sharpening?' The answer is not as simple as you might think: it depends on the condition of the edge of the tool, your experience and the supplies you have available for sharpening.

I like to start sharpening with a grit that will get the edge reshaped and restored relatively quickly. However, using a grit that is too coarse can create more work with finer grits to remove the scratches left by the coarse grit. I tend to start with a medium or fine grit and watch carefully how the edge is progressing. If it is requiring a lot of work to get close to a sharp edge, I'll step down to a coarser grit, then work my way back through progressively finer grits until I get a polished edge.

The process you use to get to a final, sharp edge is important. Each grit should remove the scratches left by the previous, coarser grit with little effort. Trying to save time by skipping from a relatively coarse grit to a very fine grit will only result in more work and disappointing results.

I recommend a minimum of four grit sizes to get the best results:

220–400 (68–35 microns)
600–1000 (26–18 microns)
1500–2000 (12–10 microns)
4000–8000 (3–1.2 microns)

If obtaining these is initially outside of your budget, the middle two grit ranges (600–2000) would be a great starting point.

With the wide range of grits from very coarse to super-fine on these diamond stones, you can handle most sharpening tasks.

Abrasive sheets

When I first started my woodworking hobby, I took the low-cost route and used wet/dry sandpaper as my sharpening medium. You can use standard sandpaper, but wet/dry sandpaper is available in a much wider range of grits and holds up well. The sandpaper sheets are readily available at most hardware stores and home centres. The finest grits (2000 and higher) can be found wherever auto body repair supplies are sold.

Abrasive sheets are available in the widest range of grits. Wet/dry sandpaper sheets are an economical option for many sharpening tasks and are a great option for beginners or if you have a tight budget. Some abrasive sheets incorporate diamond particles that are a fraction of a micron in size. These are used for polishing.

When you use wet/dry sandpaper for sharpening tools such as chisels and plane irons, it is important to have a flat surface for the abrasive sheet. You can use a piece of glass, MDF (medium-density fibreboard), or a 12 x 12in (300 x 300mm) granite tile from the home centre. Whatever you use, it should be smooth and flat.

As the name implies, wet/dry sandpaper can be used dry or with a spritz of water. I find it easier to use dry. Using water makes the paper more likely to curl, which can compromise the ability to get a properly sharpened cutting edge.

You can use tape to hold the abrasive paper down or use a light-tack spray adhesive. Once the paper is secure, you can use it to sharpen your tools.

Abrasive sheets also come in handy for other sharpening tasks. You can wrap small pieces around a pencil or dowel to sharpen gouges and other tools with a rounded cutting edge. Finer-grit sheets are ideal for touching up the edges of carving tools.

Some polishing abrasives are made with a self-adhesive polyester film backing. Adhered to a flat substrate, they make quick surfaces for polishing an edge. Yet, because of their flexibility, they also excel as a hone for curved edges.

Simple plywood bases with hardboard cleats support a piece of ¼in-thick (25mm) glass. Applying self-adhesive sandpaper or using spray adhesive with standard sandpaper creates an inexpensive, renewable sharpening stone.

This granite surface plate is designed and manufactured with tight tolerances to be used as a flat reference surface. It makes an ideal surface for using abrasive sheets as a sharpening medium.

Sharpening stones

Another abrasive that is most commonly used for sharpening jobs is in the form of a rectangular 'stone'. These natural or man-made stones come in a variety of shapes and sizes. For sharpening knives and woodworking tools such as chisels or hand plane irons, a rectangular sharpening stone is the most common form. They are available in a wide range of grit sizes.

As when using abrasive sheets on a flat substrate, it is important that the surface of the stone is flat. This ensures that the resulting edge is straight and razor sharp. It is difficult, if not impossible, to get a sharp edge when using a worn or hollowed-out stone. There are special stones available and different methods you can use to keep the stone flat.

Oil stones

When I was a young boy, my grandfather and father would often pull out an oil stone, add a few drops of lightweight oil and sharpen their pocketknives. Oil stones have been used for centuries to sharpen tools of every type.

Oil stones are natural stones that are quarried and cut to size, though manufactured versions are now available. Arkansas stones are one type of oil stone, named for the region of the United States where they are quarried. They fall into two categories: hard and soft. Soft Arkansas stones cut quickly but wear faster. Hard Arkansas stones cut more slowly and leave a more polished edge.

Oil stones work best with oil as the lubricant. Using an oil stone dry will cause it to glaze over with metal particles, which prevents the stone from cutting.

To keep an oil stone flat and remove any glazing, coarse wet/dry sandpaper on a flat surface such as glass or a granite tile will do the trick. Kerosene acts as a good cleaning and lubricating agent during the flattening process. Just place the stone face down on the sandpaper and move it in a circular motion until the face of the stone is an even colour along the

Sharpening stones like these are commonly used and readily available.

entire surface. If you have access to a coarse diamond stone, it can be used to flatten your oil stone as well.

After using an oil stone, wipe off the excess oil with a rag or paper towel. If you acquire a used oil stone or have one that is glazed over with dirt sludge, you can use a commercial product such as WD-40 and steel wool to loosen the grime. Kerosene works well also, but can be smelly and needs to be used in a well-ventilated area. For severely dirty stones, some have had success putting them in the automatic dishwasher. The detergent softens the grime, while the hot water washes it away and helps open the pores of the stone. It is important to allow the stone to cool to ambient temperature slowly to avoid cracking.

Oil stones have a centuries-old tradition of being the go-to abrasive for sharpening.

Waterstones

One popular type of sharpening stone in use today is a waterstone. It is more common to find man-made stones than natural ones, and the manufactured stones are usually less expensive. As the name suggests, waterstones work best when lubricated with water. Some stones require soaking in water several minutes before use. Others require only a spritz or two of water. It is important to follow the manufacturer's recommendations for use and care in order to prolong the life of the stone.

Waterstones can be made from a variety of abrasive particles. These abrasives are mixed with a binding agent to form the stones. This process ensures that the abrasive particles are evenly distributed throughout the stone. As the stone wears, there is no compromise in its cutting ability.

Waterstones have perhaps the widest range of grit sizes. Plus, they are noted for their fast-cutting capability. The downside to this feature is that waterstones can wear more quickly and require flattening more often. For this task, you can use coarse wet/dry sandpaper on a flat surface. You can also use an inexpensive flattening, or lapping, stone designed for this purpose. Deep grooves and aggressive grit help level the surface of a waterstone quickly. Just be sure to use plenty of water as a lubricant during the process.

While shopping for sharpening supplies, you may run across ceramic waterstones. Some people feel that ceramic waterstones last longer and wear less quickly than other types of waterstones, but this is a

Waterstones are immensely popular and available in a variety of types and grits. They are a good entry-level solution to sharpening.

Waterstones should be flattened periodically. The specialized flattening stone shown above makes quick work of levelling the surface of the waterstone.

subjective observation. This means they require flattening less often. To flatten a ceramic waterstone, a diamond plate is the best tool to use.

One manufacturer has a line of ceramic waterstones that are fused to a glass base. The glass provides a flat surface for the thin abrasive. These thinner waterstones will stay flat and are easier to store.

Waterstones are available as single-grit stones. You can also purchase dual-grit stones that feature a different grit size on each side. Dual-sided stones are an economical option and a quick way to have several grits on hand.

Caring for a waterstone means rinsing it off after every use using cold or lukewarm water. A mild dish soap and nylon-bristle brush can be used to help remove dirt and grime. Let the stones air dry before storing them. If you live in a cold climate, don't let the stones freeze or they might crack.

These waterstones utilize a ceramic abrasive fused to a flat glass panel. You use them as you would a traditional sharpening stone.

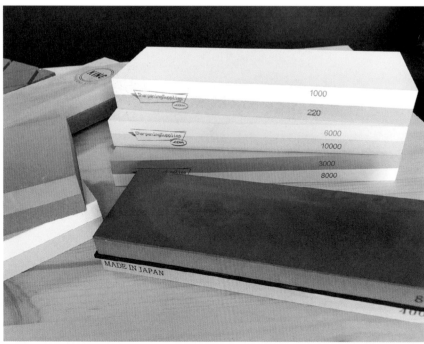

Dual-sided waterstones offer a different grit size on each side of the stone.

Diamond stones

The last category of sharpening stones I want to mention are diamond stones. These are made from man-made industrial diamond particles that are fused to a metal plate. This process has become so popular that you can find hundreds of products, from nail files to sharpening tools, that incorporate diamonds.

Some diamond stones are made by fusing diamond particles to thin plates of metal, which are then fastened to stiff plastic bases. Other stones have diamond particles fused to thick metal plates. In both cases, the end result is a long-wearing stone that never needs to be flattened. These properties alone have contributed to the immense popularity of these products.

If you take a close look at the photo below, you will see that some products have holes or patterns formed in the diamond surface. This helps prevent the slurry formed by the metal particles and lubricant – called 'swarf' – from clogging the diamond surface.

Diamond stones can be used dry, but I like to use water or a lubricant specifically designed for diamond stones. Using a diamond stone is no different than any other sharpening stone. The advantage is that you know it's going to stay flat.

To clean a diamond stone, you can use a mild detergent under running water. Use a nylon-bristle brush if needed to help remove metal particles. Dry the stone thoroughly to prevent rust. Rub a white artist's eraser over the stone to remove any remaining dirt.

When storing sharpening stones (regardless of whether they are oil stones, waterstones or diamond stones), don't stack them together where the faces are touching one another. This can transfer grit from one stone to another and cause unwanted scratches during the sharpening process. It is best to store each stone in a separate container or separated if possible. You can use an old sock to make a cushioning wrap that protects the stone during storage and transport.

Diamond sharpening products are available in numerous configurations.

Hybrid solutions

You do not have to use the same type of stone for all of your sharpening needs. Many manufacturers offer a hybrid solution that incorporates a couple of different types of stones. This allows the manufacturer to select the best stones for the task.

For example, the product shown below features two diamond stones (with coarse and fine grits) and a natural Arkansas stone. You could use the two diamond stones to quickly refine the edge and then use the Arkansas stone for putting the final polish on a razor-sharp edge.

This hybrid sharpening solution utilizes two diamond stones and an Arkansas stone mounted to a rotating base.

Stropping

A sharpening method often used to put a mirror polish on a cutting edge is known as stropping. A strop is traditionally a strip of leather. Old-fashioned barbers would use a leather strop to hone the edges of their straight razors before giving their clients a shave.

After you have used the finest sharpening stone, rub the cutting edge of the tool along the leather. This removes the finest scratches to refine the edge. It only takes a few strokes with moderate pressure. Just be sure you always pull the tool away from the cutting edge so that it doesn't dig into the leather.

You can apply a stropping compound – a waxy substance mixed with ultra-fine abrasives – to the leather to enhance this process. Simply rub the compound on the leather before stropping the tools.

Another method to strop a tool edge is to use diamond paste. These pastes come in small syringes to make it easy for you to apply to a strop. Diamond particles are mixed in a medium that you spread on a surface for stropping. This surface can be a piece of hardwood, MDF (medium-density fibreboard) or leather. I like to put a few drops of oil on the strop surface and then add just a drop or two of diamond paste. Spread it around with your finger and you're ready to touch up the edge of the tool.

Stropping with an ultra-fine abrasive puts the final polish on a cutting edge.

This strop is made by gluing a strip of leather to a plywood block. Green stropping compound provides the fine abrasive needed to obtain a polished edge.

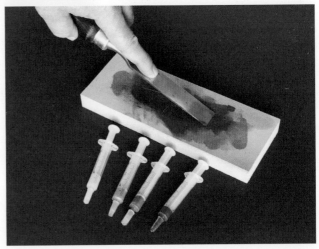

Diamond paste comes in a few grits to put the final polish on a cutting edge. Here, I'm using a block of MDF as a strop. A little diamond paste goes a long way.

Work area

Sharpening can be a messy process. After all, you're using an abrasive to remove metal, which creates a fine dust. Combine this with the oil or water you use as a lubricant, and the muddy mess can get out of hand. For this reason, I always protect the worksurface where I'll be sharpening. I like to use a silicone mat as a base for the sharpening stones. Its non-stick surface is easy to clean yet prevents the stones from sliding around during use.

Another solution that works well is an old serving tray. I found one at a charity shop that was very inexpensive. I like it because the lip around the edge contains the mess made while sharpening. It has the added benefit of keeping tools like chisels from rolling off and onto the floor accidentally.

If you're using waterstones or diamond stones, another item you'll want to have on hand is a spray bottle filled with water. I like to use distilled water because the minerals in tap water could contribute to rust on the tools. You can add a drop or two of washing-up liquid to the water. This helps lift the metal dust away from the stone and provides additional lubrication.

You'll also need rags, paper towels or disposable shop rags within easy reach. As you sharpen, you

An inexpensive silicone mat protects the worksurface and provides an easy-to-clean surface while holding sharpening stones securely in place.

need to wipe the tool clean periodically to check your progress. This has the additional benefit of removing any abrasive grit remaining on the tool that could be transferred to the next finer grit and cause unwanted scratches.

For waterstones that require soaking in water before use, a disposable plastic food container makes a good water bath. Just be sure to remove the stones to allow them to air-dry after use.

Before sharpening a tool, particularly woodworking tools, it is a good idea to determine the existing bevel angle of the tool. This helps you set up your sharpening system to maintain the same angle. There are many tools available to do this, but one of the simplest is a brass angle gauge. I keep one handy at my sharpening station.

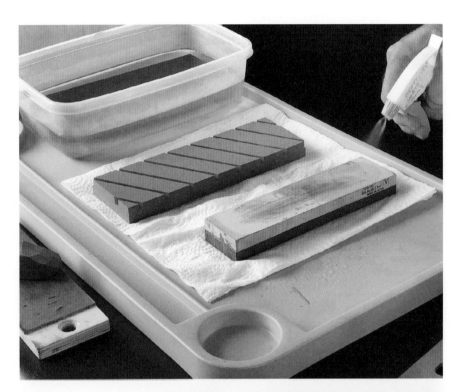

An old serving tray makes an ideal base for sharpening. It contains the mess and just takes a quick rinse to clean it after use.

Measuring the bevel angle helps you set up your sharpening system to maintain that angle. This brass gauge is a simple, inexpensive device that makes this an easy task.

Honing guides

Earlier, I talked about the geometry and importance of bevel angles when sharpening an edge (see page 16). Many beginners struggle with how to achieve a consistent bevel angle when sharpening. Even those with years of experience occasionally need to form a clean, accurate bevel on a tool.

Fortunately, there are a variety of accessories available that enable you to set and sharpen a tool like a chisel or hand plane iron with confidence.

After you set the proper angle for the bevel, these honing guides hold the blade securely to maintain that angle on a sharpening stone as you sharpen.

The simplest and least expensive honing guide is a clamp-style guide. These are available at most hardware stores and home centres. They feature a screw mechanism that, when turned, moves the jaws together to clamp the edge of the tool. The screw knob is usually slotted to provide a way for you to apply additional torque with a screwdriver to

Honing guides, or jigs, come in a variety of styles. They all serve one purpose: to set the correct angle for sharpening the bevel on chisels and plane irons.

Use the knob on a clamp-style honing guide to clamp the blade in place. The amount the blade projects determines the angle at which the tool rests on the stone.

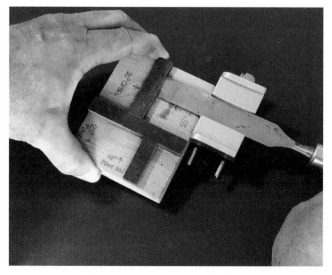

This simple jig allows you to quickly clamp a blade in a honing guide to set the proper angle for sharpening.

ensure the blade doesn't slip during use. This style of honing guide requires that the sides of the blade being clamped are parallel and relatively thin to fit the jaws of the guide. Some chisels are too thick or have tapered sides that prevent a secure grip on the blade.

Setting the proper angle of the tool to dress the bevel is done by adjusting the length of projection from the honing guide. There are a variety of ways to help you set this angle. One is to simply place the bevel of the blade flat on the stone and adjust the position of the honing guide to maintain that angle.

You can use a shop-made gauge block to help you set the angle. The one shown here features cleats that help set the correct blade projection from the honing guide.

Another way to set the angle of the blade in the honing guide is to use a digital angle gauge. The digital gauge features strong magnets to attach it to a tool blade or steel worksurface. Set it on your

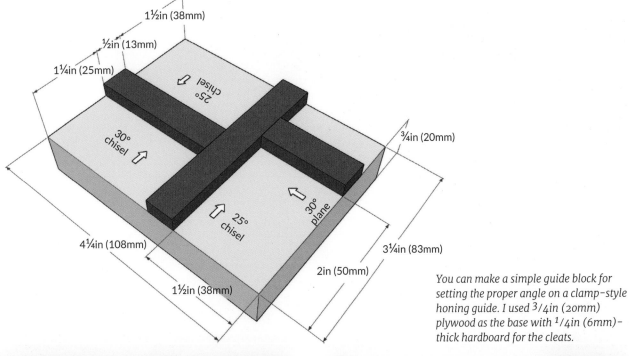

You can make a simple guide block for setting the proper angle on a clamp-style honing guide. I used 3/4in (20mm) plywood as the base with 1/4in (6mm)-thick hardboard for the cleats.

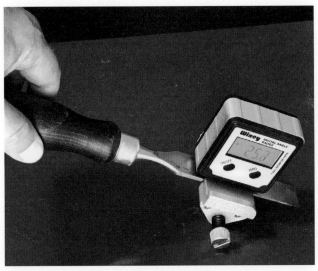

Use a digital angle gauge to quickly set the proper angle for sharpening the bevel on the tool.

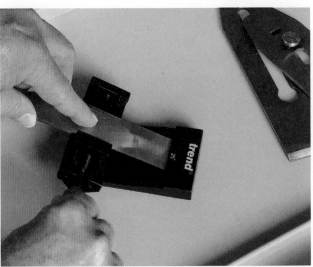

This honing guide comes with a gauge to set the blade angle. The roller of the honing guide fits in a groove in the gauge and the blade is extended to the step on the gauge indicating the desired angle.

worksurface or sharpening stone and press the 'Zero' button. Then place it on the blade in your honing guide and adjust the projection of the blade until the desired angle is displayed on the gauge.

Some honing guides come with a gauge that helps you set the blade angle with no fuss. One thing to watch for when clamping a blade in a honing guide is that the cutting edge is parallel to the roller and sits square in the guide. If the blade isn't square as you sharpen, you will be removing more material on one side of the bevel than the other, creating an uneven bevel and a skewed cutting edge. It is particularly important to make sure the blade is square on bench chisels and irons for hand planes.

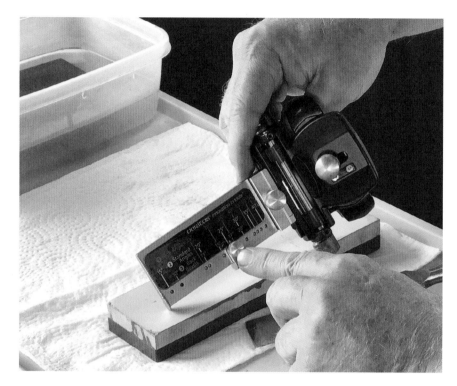

A gauge attaches to this honing guide to allow you to set a range of bevel angles for properly positioning the blade. Once the blade is securely clamped in place in the guide, you remove the gauge.

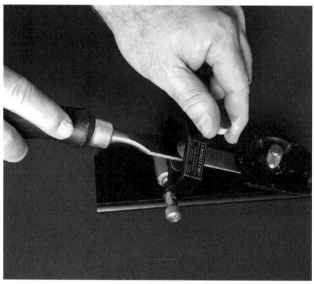

The auxiliary angle jig for this honing guide helps to position the blade not only at the proper angle for sharpening the bevel but also ensures the blade is square in the jig.

Make sure the blade is clamped square in the honing guide before you start the sharpening process.

Powered sharpeners

As you might imagine, there are many powered tools that are designed to make quick work of sharpening a blade or tool. The two most common ones you might find in a woodworking shop are bench grinders and a low-speed sharpening system by Work Sharp.

The low-speed sharpening system by Work Sharp was designed specifically for woodworking tools. It comes with a variety of accessories and features that make it ideal for sharpening and honing chisels, plane irons and carving tools.

I talk more in depth about these and other powered tools later, but these are two that anyone serious about woodworking should consider adding to their collection.

Unlike traditional bench grinders that you might find in a metalworking shop, a low-speed bench grinder is less likely to overheat the cutting edge, which can ruin the temper of the steel. It is handy for quickly reshaping and straightening an edge in addition to removing nicks.

The Work Sharp uses a low-speed motor to spin an abrasive disc. The disc is accessible from underneath, as shown here, or you can use the top of the disc to flatten chisels or hone carving tools, to name just a few examples.

2

Sharpening in practice

2:1
Chisels

While building woodworking projects, you will probably spend a fair amount of time using chisels. Proper use of a sharp chisel allows you to create and fine-tune joinery, add details to your projects and add a level of craftsmanship you cannot obtain with any other tool.

After the initial sharpening process, learning how to hone your chisels razor sharp periodically during use makes them a joy to use. Sharp chisels slice through wood fibres with less effort and leave a clean cut. Once you learn how a sharp chisel behaves in your hand, you'll know when to touch up the edge to keep it cutting smoothly.

Sharp chisels are a necessity in any woodworking shop. Knowing how to obtain a razor-sharp edge is essential for quality craftsmanship.

Flatten the back

As discussed earlier, a sharp edge is a line formed at the intersection of two flat planes (see page 16). On a chisel, these two planes are formed by the bevel and the back of the blade. Some quality tool manufacturers go the extra step of flattening, or lapping, the backs of their blades before packaging them for shipment. But chances are, if you have obtained some tools from the local hardware store or home centre, the backs of the blades have been rough-ground at the factory but aren't necessarily flat. The same holds for used tools; you can't assume that the previous owner went to the trouble of checking the back for flatness.

Flattening the back is a one-time operation you only need to perform on a newly acquired chisel, whether it's factory-new or a used one.

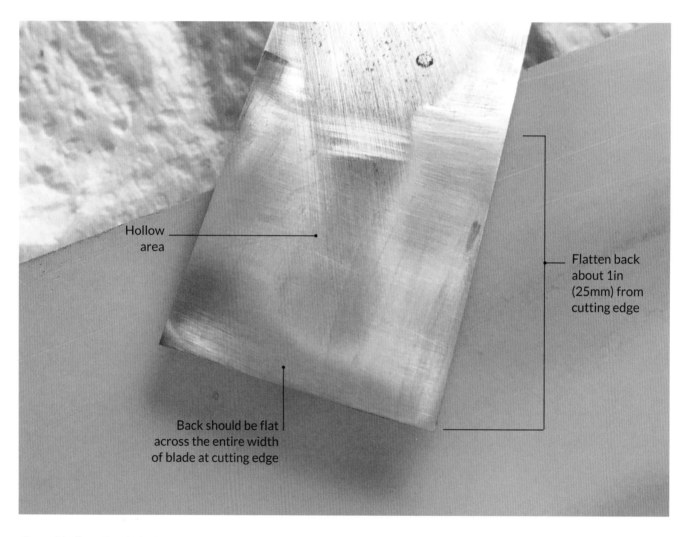

Hollow area

Flatten back about 1in (25mm) from cutting edge

Back should be flat across the entire width of blade at cutting edge

The goal in flattening the back is to get a consistent scratch pattern all the way across the width of the blade closest to the cutting edge. Work through finer grits to a polished surface.

The goal is to polish the back of the blade to a mirror finish.

Before you start to work on flattening the back, it's important to point out a couple of things. First, we're only concerned with the area on the back of the blade close to the cutting edge. I usually focus on flattening the back no more than about ¾–1in (20–25mm) from the edge. This provides enough surface to keep the chisel flat on the sharpening stone. It is not necessary to flatten the entire length of the chisel back.

The second thing to point out is that the back of the chisel should be flat all the way to the cutting edge. In other words, you need to be careful not to round over the edge when flattening the back. This can happen unintentionally if the back of the chisel doesn't sit flat on the sharpening stone as you go through the flattening process.

If there is a rounded edge or slight bevel on the back of the chisel, opposite the bevel side, it essentially renders the chisel useless for most woodworking tasks. The reason is that the back of

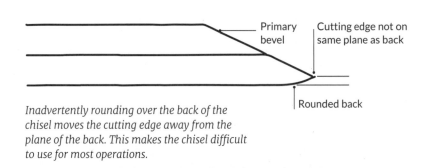

Primary bevel

Cutting edge not on same plane as back

Rounded back

Inadvertently rounding over the back of the chisel moves the cutting edge away from the plane of the back. This makes the chisel difficult to use for most operations.

Keeping the back of the blade flat on the stone, make repeated strokes across the length of the stone until an even scratch pattern appears across the width of the blade at the cutting edge.

the chisel serves as a reference face for the cutting edge. A rounded edge on the back essentially moves the cutting edge away from the plane of the back.

With that in mind, I like to start flattening the back using a coarse grit stone (220–400 grit). Position the stone close and parallel to the front edge of the workbench or worksurface.

The key to this operation is hand placement on the chisel as you polish the back on the sharpening stone. I like to use my dominant hand wrapped around the blade (not the handle) close to the cutting edge, with my index finger applying pressure downward at the bevel end, keeping the back flat on the stone. My other index finger applies downward pressure on the blade.

The key is to never lift the back end (handle) of the chisel during the flattening process. Holding the chisel on the blade close to the bevel end instead of the handle end reduces this temptation. Make sure there is nothing on the workbench holding the handle end of the chisel up, preventing the back of the chisel from resting flat on the stone. Once you are certain the back is flat on the stone, make strokes along the length of the stone while keeping pressure downward on the bevel end to keep the blade flat.

Check your progress periodically by wiping the back with a rag or paper towel. You should start to see a scratch pattern or shiny spots in the metal. This shows you where the high spots are. If you have trouble seeing this, a trick I use is to mark the back of the blade with a permanent marker. After colouring in the area near the edge, a few strokes on the stone will remove the marker at the high spots. Keep up the flattening process on the coarse stone until the back is flat right near the cutting edge.

Some blades will have a hollow, or concave, area behind the cutting edge. This is somewhat common and is of no concern. Just keep working the back until the hollow is worked away from the cutting edge.

Japanese-style chisels are made from laminated steel and are intentionally made with a deep hollow area on the back of the blade that makes them easier to flatten.

If you have a blade that is crowned, or convex, on the back, it is a bit more challenging to get flat. If this is the case, I use the coarsest stone available and try to hold the blade in one position to keep it from rocking from side to side during the flattening process. Depending on the amount of crown, it could take a fair amount of effort to get the back of the

Marking the back of the blade with a permanent marker before starting the flattening process allows you to quickly determine where the high and low spots are located. You can apply the marker periodically to help gauge your progress.

blade flat. Sometimes a power sharpener that uses abrasive discs or belts can be of assistance here to remove the bulk of the high area. A coarse diamond stone works well too.

Once the back is flat all the way across the width right at the cutting edge, you can step up to the next finest abrasive. Work your way through the finer abrasives to remove scratch patterns from the previous grit. It is a good idea to wipe the blade between grits to keep from transferring a coarse grit to the finer grit. I like to polish the back through at least 2000-grit. Remember, this is a one-time operation. As you progress through the grits, you are removing scratches left by the coarser grit. Polishing the back to a mirror finish will help create a sharper cutting edge.

Japanese-style chisels are made with a hollow back to make flattening the back less labour-intensive.

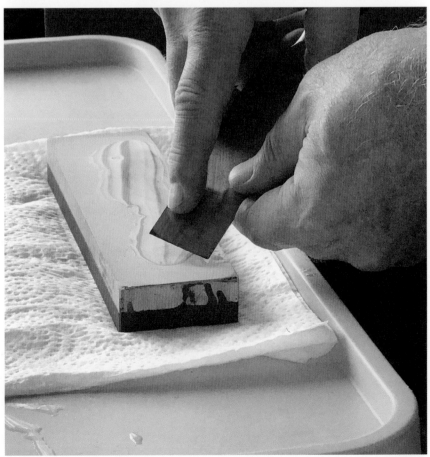

Check your progress often as you flatten the back. Once the scratch pattern reaches all the way across the width of the blade right at the cutting edge, you can move on to finer grits to obtain a polished surface.

Hone the bevelled edge

After the back is flat and polished, you can turn your attention to the bevel. Like the back, you are only concerned with the area nearest the cutting edge. It is not always necessary to polish the entire bevel. Again, with higher-quality chisels, the bevels have already been lapped flat, so all you need to do is polish the bevel to hone the cutting edge before you are ready to put the chisel to use.

The bevels on some less expensive chisels are ground at the factory with a coarse grinding wheel. This leaves deep scratches that must be removed.

This rough grinding process can also create what is commonly called a hollow grind. This is the result of the outer diameter of the wheel grinding away metal in the form of a slight arc on the bevel. This can make the sharpening process easier since there are only two points of contact on the sharpening stone. Contrast this with a flat bevel where the entire surface of the bevel is to be polished.

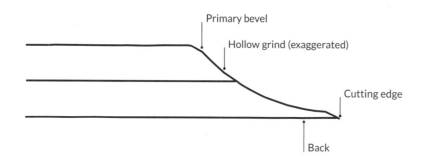

Primary bevel

Hollow grind (exaggerated)

Cutting edge

Back

The bevels on some chisels are ground at the factory with a grinding wheel that leaves a concave surface. Honing the bevel is easy because the top of the bevel (heel) and the cutting edge (toe) are the only two points of contact with the stone.

Some chisels are ground with a rough grinding wheel at the factory. These deep scratches must be removed from the back and bevel at the cutting edge.

Using a honing guide

For most beginners, it helps to use a honing guide to sharpen the bevel. A honing guide holds the blade at a consistent angle and maintains a square edge. Wheels or rollers help the honing guide move back and forth along the length of the stone or abrasive. Your job is to apply light pressure at the cutting edge to sharpen the edge.

Honing guides vary widely in cost. Some clamp the blade at the sides, and you're left to determine the angle at which the bevel contacts the stone. The amount the blade extends from the honing guide sets the angle. This isn't as hard as it might sound, but it can be a trial-and-error process at first.

With the blade clamped in the honing guide, it is a good idea to make sure the blade is square to the guide. While some chisels, like skew chisels, are designed with angled cutting edges, the cutting edges on bench chisels should be square. Keeping a small square handy near your sharpening station is helpful.

Secure the blade in the honing guide and place the guide on the sharpening stone. Sight under the bevel, then adjust the blade projection until the bevel is resting flat on the stone. Some more advanced honing guides come with jigs and accessories that help set the angle with little fuss.

Before honing the bevel, use a small square to make sure the chisel is clamped square in the honing guide.

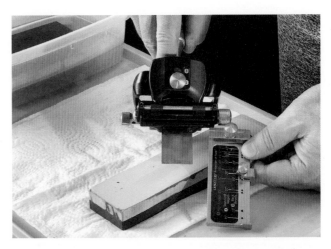

This honing guide features an angle registration jig that sets the angle for the bevel.

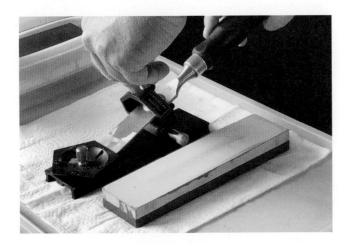

This honing guide features an accessory that allows you to quickly set standard bevel angles in the honing guide.

With the blade clamped in a simple, side-clamping-style honing guide, adjust the position until the bevel sits flat on the stone.

Bevel angles

This would be a good time to mention bevel angles on chisels. The most common bevel angle for bench chisels is 25°. This can vary a few degrees depending on the manufacturer. Paring chisels, which are designed to slice easily through end grain, feature a 20° or lower bevel. Paring chisels are designed to be used with hand pressure only, since the cutting edge is weaker because of the shallower bevel. Mortise chisels, on the other hand, take a lot of pressure and beating with a mallet to remove waste from a mortise. Their bevel angles are around 30°. You can use the illustration below to estimate the bevel angle of your chisels.

Once you have the blade secured in the honing guide, it is time to start honing the edge. The grit you start with depends on the condition of the bevel. If the cutting edge is not square to the sides of the chisel or is damaged, you will want to start with the coarsest grit to re-establish a square, straight cutting edge. From there, work your way up through the grits.

When honing, take advantage of the full length of the stone. If you are using a honing guide, make sure the roller on the guide and the bevel on the blade remain on the stone.

As you did when flattening the back, you can use a permanent marker to help gauge your progress. It is especially helpful for highlighting whether you are applying even pressure across the cutting edge.

30°
25°
20°
15°
0°

Common bevel angles

The sharpening process is the same regardless of the honing guide you choose. Use the entire length of the stone and make smooth, even strokes back and forth while applying moderate pressure to the cutting edge.

A marker is helpful in determining your progress as you hone the bevel.

Freehand sharpening

As you gain experience with sharpening, you may want to try honing your chisels freehand, without the use of a honing guide. It is not as difficult as it may seem. The benefit of freehand sharpening is that it saves time and the hassle of setting up the proper angle on a honing guide. For quick touch-ups, it is fast and easy.

The trick to honing without the use of a guide is to learn to 'feel the bevel'. To do this, place the blade bevel-down on the stone. Rock the blade back until it is resting on the heel of the bevel. Then slowly lift the handle of the chisel until you feel the flat of the bevel contact the stone. If you are using a lubricant such as oil or water, you can watch the edge of the chisel and see a bead of liquid form as the cutting edge contacts the stone.

From here, it is a matter of maintaining that angle as you slide the blade across the stone. You may have to experiment to find out how to position your hands and fingers to keep downward pressure on the bevel. For me, I wrap one hand around the blade, extending my index finger to the tip to keep the bevel flat on the stone. For narrow chisels, this is adequate. For wider chisels, I use the index finger of my other hand to help keep the blade stable on the stone.

When sharpening by hand without the aid of a guide, it is important not to rock the blade as you make strokes along the stone. To avoid this, I like to place the stone so the long edge is facing away from me. I'll place the cutting edge parallel to the long edge of the stone and make strokes on the stone away from and towards my body.

Another method for freehand sharpening is to orient the blade so that it is perpendicular to the long edge of the stone. Using two hands, you move the blade away from and towards you. The difficulty with this method is that there is a tendency to inadvertently change the bevel angle as you move the blade away from you. Therefore, I prefer orienting the blade sideways and making strokes parallel with the cutting edge.

Find the hand position that works best for you to keep the bevel flat on the stone as you make strokes along the length of the stone.

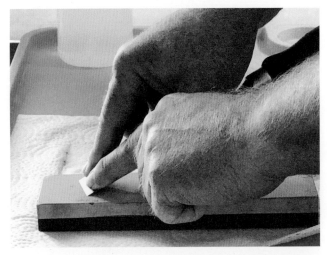

Using two hands to hold the blade in this orientation is difficult without some experience. There is a tendency to rock the bevel, which can create a rounded bevel surface.

Remove the burr

As you hone the bevel and work your way through finer grits, you may see a wire edge or burr form at the cutting edge. This happens as the cutting edge gets thinner and thinner and the metal is forced to the back side of the bevel, forming a burr. This happens often and is perfectly normal. It is a sign that you're making good progress towards a sharp edge.

To remove the burr, all you need to do is place the back of the blade flat on the finest stone you're using and make one stroke away from the cutting edge. Just make sure the back is flat on the stone as you do this.

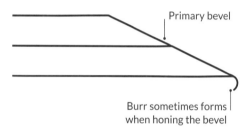

Primary bevel

Burr sometimes forms
when honing the bevel

A 'wire edge' or burr often forms on the cutting edge as you hone the bevel. This is easy to remove on a fine stone or strop.

At the end of the sharpening process, it's a good idea to remove any burr. To do this, place the back of the blade on a fine stone or strop and pull away from the cutting edge. It only takes one or two strokes.

Stropping

At this point your chisel is probably ready to use. However, some people like to go one step further and strop the edge. This puts a final polish on the bevel to create the keenest edge.

Stropping involves using a compound that contains fine abrasives. The stropping or polishing compound is applied to a substrate such as leather or a flat piece of wood. A piece of leather glued to plywood makes a handy strop. You can find leather wherever sharpening or leathercraft supplies are sold. You can even use an old, wide leather belt.

To strop the edge of a chisel, apply the compound to the leather. I like to use the smooth side of the leather. Place the bevel of the tool down on the strop and use firm pressure to pull the blade in the direction away from the cutting edge. It is easy to cut into the strop if you're not careful when repositioning the blade between strokes. Lift the chisel at the end of the stroke, then reposition it at the opposite end for each stroke. After sharpening a chisel on stones, I will usually give the bevel about twenty strokes on the strop. Then, to remove any burr, I place the back on the strop and pull away from the cutting edge.

A strop uses an ultra-fine abrasive or polishing compound to create a polished edge.

Secondary or micro-bevel

Trying to keep the entire face of the bevel flat and true can be a chore, so many opt instead to create a secondary bevel, or micro-bevel, along the cutting edge. This requires fewer strokes when sharpening and is a quick way to obtain a sharp edge.

A secondary bevel is formed by adjusting the angle of the blade only a few degrees. I do this on the finest stone. It only takes a few strokes to create this secondary bevel. If you look at the cutting edge closely, you'll be able to see a fine line where this bevel is formed. From here you can proceed to the stropping operation as before.

Touching up the secondary bevel as your chisel becomes dull is faster and easier than polishing the entire primary bevel. As you continuously sharpen your chisel by polishing the secondary bevel, you'll gradually widen this bevel. At some point you will want to re-establish the primary bevel. This is best done using a honing guide.

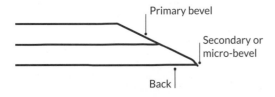

A secondary bevel makes sharpening faster and easier, plus it strengthens the cutting edge.

A finely honed, polished edge is ready to put to work.

Test for sharpness

There are a variety of ways you can check the cutting edge for sharpness. Some try shaving the hair of their arm. I don't recommend this for safety reasons. I check the edge against the smooth surface of the back of my thumbnail. If the blade catches on it instead of slipping, I can be certain the edge is sharp. If the blade is dull, it will skate across my nail without grabbing.

A better test for sharpness is to try to shave the end grain of a softwood like pine or cedar. You should be able to slice a thin shaving. If you find the blade is crushing the fibres instead of cleanly slicing them, you have more work to do to hone the edge.

See if the cutting edge 'catches' on your thumbnail with light pressure. If it tends to slip off, the edge needs a little more honing.

If your chisel can make curls by slicing the end grain of a softwood, you have accomplished the goal of getting the edge razor sharp.

Mortise chisels

Mortise chisels are designed to take a lot of pounding with a mallet to chop out waste from a mortise. There is a lot of force applied at the cutting edge. Because of this, mortise chisels feature a much thicker steel for the blade. A benefit of this is that it creates a wide bevel that makes a mortise chisel easier to sharpen freehand if you feel comfortable doing so.

If you wish to use a honing guide, you might have some difficulty. Because of the thicker blade, the chisel can't be clamped securely in most honing guides. The Veritas Mk.II Narrow Blade Honing Guide has an accessory mortise blade attachment that you can purchase that enables the honing guide to clamp a mortise chisel.

The process for sharpening a mortise chisel is the same as the standard bench chisel we discussed before (see pages 50–59). It is important to make sure the back is flat right up near the cutting edge. Then you can focus on the bevel.

The bevel angle of a mortise chisel from the manufacturer may be at 25°, but because of the constant force from a mallet, most woodworkers like to form a secondary bevel closer to 30°. This effectively beefs up the cutting edge while still providing a sharp edge to cut through tough wood fibres.

Once the bevel is honed and the edge is nice and sharp, some woodworkers skip the polishing and stropping steps on a mortise chisel. After all, it is a tool designed for roughing out a cavity in the wood. On the other hand, some think that polishing and stropping a mortise chisel makes it cut faster and cleaner. Whatever the case, a mortise chisel is likely to require more frequent sharpening due to the constant impact force from a mallet that transfers to the cutting edge.

Mortise chisels feature thicker blades that create a wide bevel for sharpening.

Sharpening a mortise chisel follows the same process as sharpening a standard bench chisel. Flatten the back, then hone the bevelled edge.

Skew chisels

Skew chisels are specialized tools that feature an angled cutting edge. They excel at slicing and paring operations as well as being able to reach tight into corners.

When beginners look at a skewed blade for the first time, they can be intimidated at the thought of sharpening it. After all, it is important to maintain both the angle of the cutting edge as well as the bevel angle. In reality, it is no different than sharpening a standard chisel. The trick is the method you use to hold the blade during the sharpening process.

A foolproof jig I like to use is the Skew Registration Jig for the Veritas Mk.II Honing Guide. It allows you to determine the proper skew angle and bevel angle at the same time. Then you can clamp the blade in the honing guide, maintaining those angles.

You can also sharpen a skew chisel freehand. The tricky part is making sure the bevel is flat on the stone. You may have to experiment with the proper hand position to make sure the bevel and skew angles are maintained. It's not that difficult with a little practice.

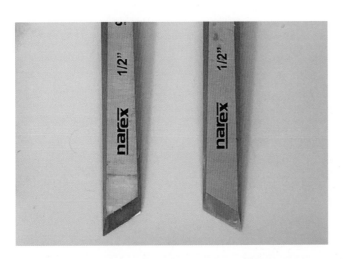

Sharpening a skew chisel doesn't need to be intimidating. The trick is to make sure the face of the bevel maintains contact with the sharpening stone.

With the skewed blade held securely in a honing guide, follow the same sharpening process as before.

The Veritas Skew Registration Jig takes the frustration out of clamping a skewed blade in a honing guide.

Freehand sharpening eliminates the hassle of using a honing guide or jig to hold the blade. Once you figure out the proper hand position to keep the bevel flat on the stone, it's easy work.

Power sharpening

If you find that sharpening chisels by hand is a tedious process, especially if you do a lot of sharpening, you might want to consider a powered sharpening solution. There are a myriad of machines and devices that you can purchase.

Bench grinder

One of the more common tools people think of for sharpening is a bench grinder. I don't recommend the typical bench grinder for sharpening tools; they are designed for metalworking shops that need to remove a lot of material quickly. A standard bench grinder typically runs at 3500RPM or higher. It takes a lot of practice and experience to use a bench grinder for sharpening tools. Friction during the grinding process builds up heat. Too much heat can damage and soften the steel at the cutting edge. It is important to keep the blade cool while sharpening.

Instead, I look for low-speed grinders that run at 1750RPM or slower. These still generate heat, but the temperature rise is slower and easier to manage. This helps keep the blade cooler. It is a good idea to keep a container of water nearby to help cool the blade in case it gets too hot. If the metal is too hot to handle comfortably, it is best to dip it in cool water.

The second consideration when using a grinder is abrasive options. A standard grinder comes with very coarse grinding wheels that are designed to cut quickly. They are great for grinding out nicks and damage to the cutting edge, but are too coarse for sharpening needs. Instead, opt for 120-grit or higher wheels.

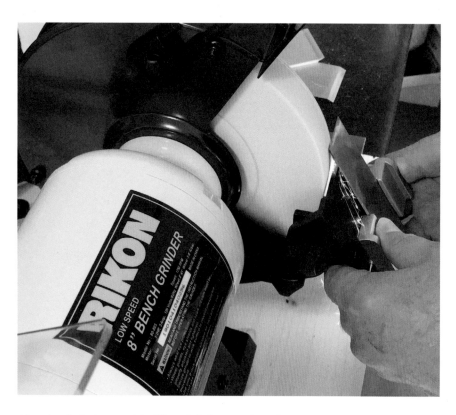

A bench grinder is a great tool for redefining a cutting edge. It is important to make sure the tool doesn't get too hot.

You can also purchase compressed paper or hard felt wheels for a bench grinder. They are more appropriate for refining an edge and are used with a polishing compound to create a razor-sharp edge on the tool.

Work Sharp

Another popular option for sharpening tools is the Work Sharp WS3000. It's a low-speed (580RPM) sharpener that uses self-adhesive abrasive discs mounted on wheels. Glass wheels allow you to mount an abrasive disc on each side. Also included is a slotted plastic wheel used to sharpen carving tools where you need to monitor the sharpening progress on the cutting edge. The Work Sharp also features an adjustable angled tool port for holding chisels and blade irons at a consistent angle.

The Work Sharp's flat, glass wheel makes it ideal for lapping the backs of chisels and plane irons flat.

You can start with a coarse abrasive disc and progress through finer grits until the back is flat and polished.

If you check out retailers online that stock woodworking and carving tools, you will find dozens of options for sharpening chisels. Choose one that fits your budget and learn to use it effectively. After a little practice, you'll soon appreciate the ease with which a sharp chisel cuts.

The Work Sharp system makes touching up the bevel a breeze.

The Work Sharp eliminates the drudgery of flattening the backs of chisels.

2:2
Hand planes

In my opinion, there is no more accurate tool in the woodworking shop than a sharp hand plane. Properly sharpened and tuned, a hand plane can remove whisper-thin shavings to fine-tune joinery or create a silky smooth surface ready for a finish.

In this section I will discuss how to sharpen irons for a variety of planes. The good news is that a lot of the techniques and supplies used for sharpening plane irons are just like those used for chisels. Refer to the previous chapter for a refresher about how to flatten the back of the iron, hone the bevel and create a micro-bevel. All that information also applies to hand planes.

A sharp hand plane is a joy to use.
Proper sharpening and set-up are key.

Bevel up or bevel down?

When we talk about sharpening hand planes, it helps to know the orientation of the iron in the plane's body. Most traditional bench planes, like the top illustration shown below, are used with the iron bevel down. The typical bevel angle is around 25°. The iron is bedded in the plane at approximately 45°, which means the cutting edge engages the wood at that same angle.

On a bevel-down plane, the bevel angle can vary slightly and not affect the overall angle of attack when planing. The cutting edge is referenced off the back of the iron, opposite the bevel. This makes the exact bevel angle of the iron less critical than that of a bevel-up configuration, as we'll see below. Be careful, though: too high a bevel angle (approaching 30° or more) can cause the heel of the bevel to ride on the wood, lifting the cutting edge too high to engage the wood and preventing it from cutting.

Some planes are manufactured so that the bevel on the iron is facing up. This bevel-up configuration changes the angle of attack to a lower angle. The lower photo below shows a cutaway of a modern hand plane with a low-angle, bevel-up configuration.

As you can see in the photo, the blade is bedded at a much lower angle – in this case, 12°. If the bevel angle of the iron is 25°, this makes the angle of attack on the wood a lower 37° than the 45° on a standard bench plane. This makes it excel at slicing the wood fibres, especially on end grain.

For low-angle, bevel-up planes, you can often purchase other irons with higher bevel angles. For example, an iron with a 38° bevel makes a 50° overall cutting angle, closer to that of a bevel-down bench plane. For this reason, a low-angle, bevel-up configuration in a hand plane makes it a more versatile tool.

How does a bevel-up or bevel-down plane affect the sharpening process? It doesn't – with one exception that I'll mention later. You still need to flatten the back and sharpen the bevel.

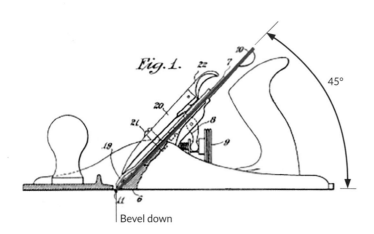

Fig. 1.

45°

Bevel down

This early 20th-century US patent drawing shows a typical bench plane with the bevel on the blade (highlighted in red) facing down.

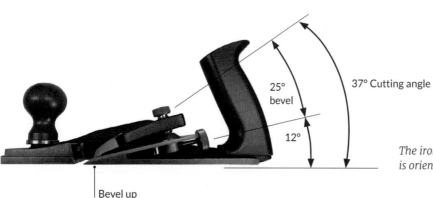

25° bevel

12°

37° Cutting angle

Bevel up

The iron (highlighted in red) on this low-angle plane is oriented with the bevel up.

Sharpening bench plane irons

As with chisels, the first thing to check on a plane iron is the flatness of the back. I use a permanent marker to colour the back side of the iron about 1in (25mm) back from the cutting edge. This provides a visual reference and shows where material is being removed as you rub the iron on the abrasive sharpening media.

The plane iron shown in the photo below came from the factory with a hollow, concave area on the back face. Starting with coarse-grit sharpening stones and working through finer grits, I was eventually able to get the cutting edge flat and polished all the way across. If the iron has a high (convex) spot in the middle, I recommend returning it or, in the case of an old plane, replacing it with a new iron. It takes too much work to remove a high area and work towards a flat surface.

In the bottom photo you can see how the iron on a Japanese hand plane is purposely hollowed out on the back side. Similar to Japanese chisels, this makes it much easier to flatten the back at the cutting edge since there is less material to remove.

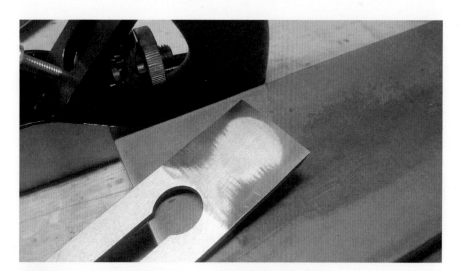

The back of this iron is flat where it counts the most − right at the cutting edge.

Japanese plane irons are made with a hollow back, which facilitates flattening.

Remember that flattening the back is a one-time operation. I like to work through finer and finer grits until a mirror polish is achieved. I do this on an 8000-grit or 10000-grit waterstone. Use the highest grit you have; you can always polish to a higher grit later.

A flat back establishes the first plane of sharpness, as discussed earlier (see page 50). Now you can turn your attention to sharpening the bevel.

The bevel on most bevel-down bench planes is 25°, but you'll want to verify this before you set the blade in a honing guide.

With the iron securely clamped in the honing guide, you're ready to start sharpening. For a new plane iron that might have grinding marks from the factory, I'll start with a relatively coarse grit (200- to 400-grit). Once the grinding scratches are removed, start moving up through progressively finer grits until the bevel is polished. Be sure to wipe the blade clean before moving up to the next grit – you don't want to transfer a coarse grit to a finer stone.

When the scratches are removed from the previous grit, you can move up to the next finer grit.

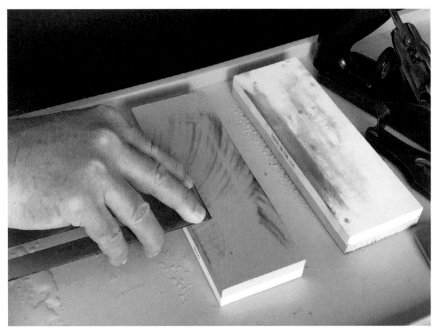

Working your way up through finer grits will create a polished surface.

Here, I'm setting the bevel angle on the honing guide to sharpen the bevel on a plane iron. Follow the instructions for your honing guide for this operation.

Check your progress frequently. There's no harm in stepping back to a coarser grit if you find the scratches aren't coming out relatively quickly. Then you can work your way back up to a fine polish.

If your chisel or plane iron is ground with a standard 25° or 30° bevel angle, you can use the FastTrack honing jig shown on page 70. It's a little unconventional because you hold the blade stationary while moving a carriage back and forth to move a small diamond stone across the bevel.

Think of it as a honing guide and sharpening stone all in one unit. This jig uses small, replaceable diamond stones in various grits to hone the bevel.

The honing guide also features a flat area with a diamond coating that's designed to remove any burr from the back of the blade that may form while sharpening the bevel.

Use the full length of the sharpening stone while applying even pressure across the width of the blade, keeping the bevel in contact with the stone.

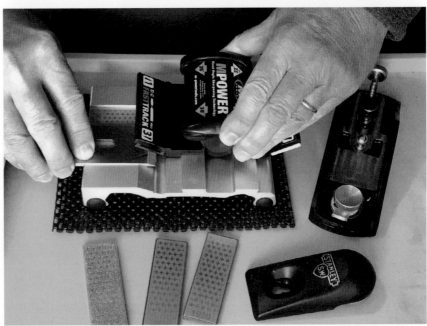

This honing jig uses a sliding carriage to move a diamond stone across the bevel of a blade.

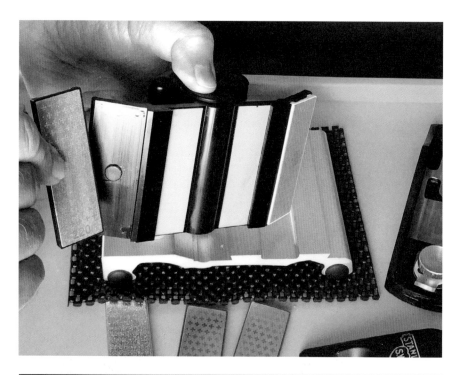

This FastTrack honing jig from MPower utilizes small diamond stones that snap into place with magnets.

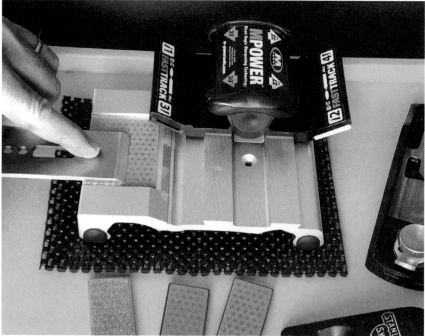

With the blade flat on the diamond surface on the jig, pull it back away from the cutting edge to remove any burr.

Forming a micro-bevel

If you wish to form a micro-bevel, or secondary bevel, on a plane iron, there are a couple of ways to go about it. With the sharpening jig shown opposite, the diamond stones are wedge-shaped to angle the stone at 2.5°. Depending on the orientation of the stone, you can form a 2.5° or 5° micro-bevel just by swapping the position of the stone in the jig.

Some conventional, older-style honing guides provide a mechanism for creating a micro-bevel.

For me, I find that forming a micro-bevel is just as quick and easy to do by hand. To do this, place the iron on the sharpening stone and rock it on the bevel until you feel the bevel sitting flat on the stone. Then just lift the back end of the iron ever so slightly (a degree or two) and make about six strokes across the stone. It doesn't take much.

I like to form a micro-bevel freehand on the sharpening stone. I hold the blade as shown and make a few strokes along the length of the stone.

Freehand sharpening

Once I have the bevel on a plane iron nice and flat with a straight cutting edge, I typically perform most of my sharpening freehand, without the aid of a honing guide. That thought may scare you a bit, but with some practice, you'll find that touching up the edge of a blade this way is quick and easy. By the time you fuss around trying to get the blade clamped in a honing guide, you could have sharpened the blade by hand and been back to work.

There are several methods of holding the iron you can use. One is to use two hands, as shown below.

The method shown here, with the cutting edge of the iron parallel to the ends of the sharpening stone, can be difficult for some. There is a tendency to rock the iron as you extend your arms. It takes practice to maintain the same orientation and angle of the iron as you sharpen.

Use two hands to keep the bevel of the plane iron flat on the stone throughout the stroke. Try not to rock the iron, which would round over the edge.

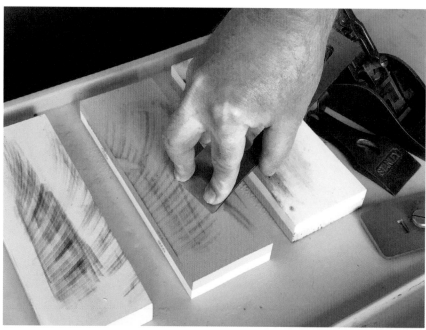

Orientating the cutting edge of the iron parallel with the long edges of the sharpening stone helps to keep the bevel flat on the stone as you sharpen.

Another method, and one that I find myself using the most, is to orient the iron sideways, so the cutting edge is more parallel with the long sides of the sharpening stone.

Japanese plane irons are quite thick compared to their Western counterparts. Some irons are forged by hand so there can be irregularities in the thickness. Plane irons may also be wedge-shaped, tapering in thickness along their length. All these reasons make it difficult to use a honing guide. The only option is to sharpen them freehand.

Fortunately, freehand sharpening with a Japanese plane iron is easier than with the thinner iron found on most Western-style hand planes. The additional thickness of the iron makes the bevel extra wide. This provides plenty of surface to keep the bevel flat on the sharpening stone.

Once you have the bevel polished, you can decide if you want to form a micro-bevel. The process for doing this is the same. Simply lift the top end of the iron a degree or two and make half a dozen or so strokes along the stone.

The extra thickness on a Japanese plane iron creates a wide bevel that is easier to sharpen using freehand techniques.

With the bevel of a Japanese plane iron flat on the sharpening stone, make strokes along the entire length of the stone, keeping the bevel flat.

Creating a cambered edge

Most woodworkers like to form a slight curve, or camber, on the cutting edge of their plane irons, particularly on traditional, bevel-down smoothing planes. This camber is an almost imperceptible radius. It amounts to removing a few thousandths of an inch at the corners of the cutting edge.

The reason for creating a cambered edge is to allow the plane to create a smooth surface without the corners of the iron digging in and causing plane

tracks. A cambered edge creates a thicker shaving in the centre that tapers to a thinner shaving at the outside edges. Bear in mind, this is on a microscopic level and is difficult to see with the naked eye. After making overlapping strokes with the plane to smooth a wide board, for example, these small changes in shaving thickness aren't visible to the naked eye and the resulting surface feels silky smooth to the touch.

A cambered plane iron enables you to plane a wide surface to a glass-smooth finish.

With the plane iron in the honing guide, apply pressure to one corner and make approximately six to ten strokes.

Creating a cambered edge is easier than you might think. As a matter of fact, I learned the hard way that it is easy to create too much of a camber. Here's my technique that makes it foolproof.

The process simply involves applying more pressure on one side of the iron for a few strokes. I do this on a fine stone. Then repeat the process with the same number of strokes on the opposite corner.

For new plane irons, I perform one more step – I take a coarse sharpening stone or fine file and knock off the sharp corners of the iron. It just takes a few light strokes. Doing this helps prevent those 'plane tracks' I talked about earlier where the corners of the iron leave ridges in the wood surface as you're planing.

When creating a camber on an iron for a bevel-up plane, there is one thing to keep in mind. Due to the geometry of the bevel angle and its orientation to the wood, you need to exaggerate the amount of camber to have the same effect as the smaller camber on a bevel-down configuration. All this means is a few more strokes on the sharpening stone while applying pressure at each corner.

Repeating the process on the opposite edge of the plane iron creates the slightest cambered edge.

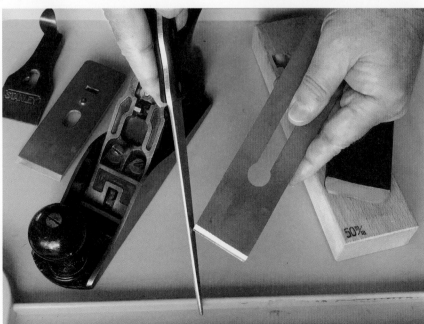

Use a file to knock the sharp corners off a new plane iron. Go easy – it just takes a few strokes.

Stropping

To put the final polished edge on their plane irons, some woodworkers will go the extra step and use a stropping compound. I use a piece of leather glued to a plywood block. After applying the green compound, make fifteen or twenty strokes with the bevel down, only pulling the iron towards you with moderate pressure. Make sure to lift the iron between strokes to prevent cutting into the leather accidentally.

Stropping the plane iron creates a mirror polish and razor-sharp edge.

Rebate and shoulder plane irons

A shoulder plane or rebate (rabbet) plane is a great addition to the woodworker's toolbox. When properly sharpened and tuned, it excels at fine-tuning the fit of joints like tenons, dados, rebates and grooves.

To sharpen the iron, it follows the same route as a standard plane iron. For this, I like to use a honing guide. Doing this helps ensure that the cutting edge remains square to the sides of the iron. This is critical to get the best performance from the plane.

Some honing guides may have trouble clamping the odd-shaped blade of a shoulder plane. If that's the case, you can resort to freehand sharpening using a little care.

Like other plane irons or chisels, you can decide if you want to take the extra step of forming a micro-bevel and stropping the edge.

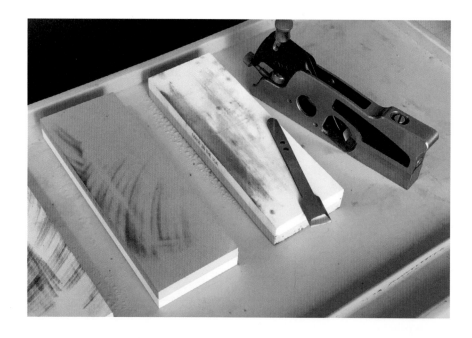

Sharpening the iron for a shoulder plane isn't difficult; it just takes a little extra care to make sure the cutting edge is square.

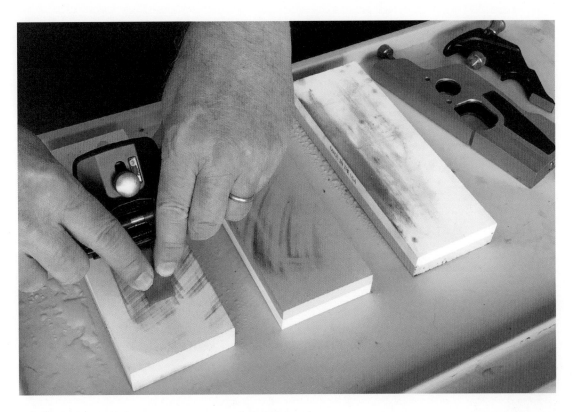

A honing guide helps hold the blade securely to hone the bevel square to the sides of the iron.

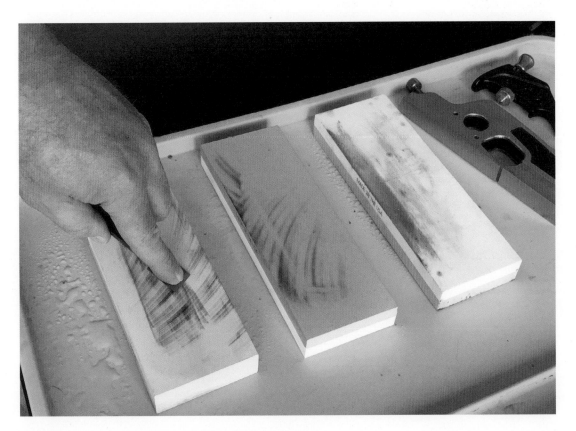

Sharpening an iron for a shoulder plane simply means using care to apply even pressure along the bevel as you sharpen. It takes a little practice to get the right technique.

Spokeshave blades

A spokeshave comes in handy in the workshop when forming rounded shapes like chair rungs or curved rails for a table. The iron in the spokeshave resembles a plane iron except that it is much shorter.

You'll want to go through the process of making sure the back of the iron is flat, just as before. You should aim for a mirror polish. Once that's done, you can focus on the bevel.

Because the iron is shorter than an iron on a bench plane, it may not clamp securely in some

styles of honing guides. It may be easier to sharpen the iron using freehand techniques. The trick is holding the bevel at a consistent angle against the stone as you sharpen. This is why I prefer the side-to-side motion along the length of the stone, as shown below.

After the bevel is polished, turn the iron over with the back of the cutting edge flat on the stone. Make one or two strokes away from the cutting edge to remove any burr.

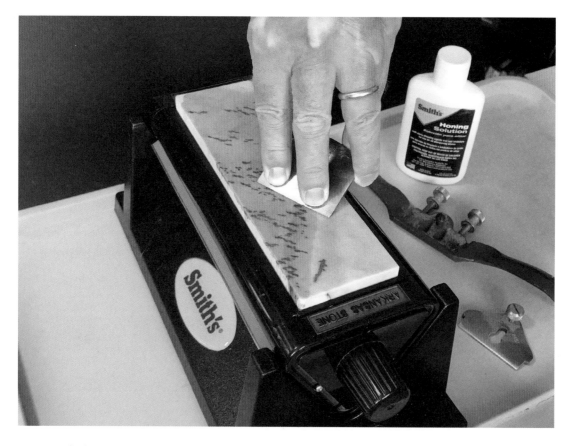

Treat a spokeshave iron just like the iron on a traditional hand plane.

Skewed blades

Some hand planes designed especially for joinery will have a skewed blade. All this means is that the cutting edge is formed at an angle to the sides of the iron rather than being square (see photo below).

Some honing guides aren't designed to clamp a skewed blade securely. Even if they are, setting the proper bevel at the same time as the correct skew angle can be frustrating. There are a couple of ways around this. The first is to use a specialized skew attachment for the honing guide.

After the iron is clamped securely in the honing guide and you have double-checked that the bevel sits flat on the sharpening stone, you're ready to sharpen. The process is the same as with a chisel or plane iron except that there is no camber to the edge.

Of course, if you have difficulty using a honing guide, you can sharpen the skewed iron freehand. As I mentioned before, it's all about keeping the bevel flat on the stone as you sharpen (see page 57).

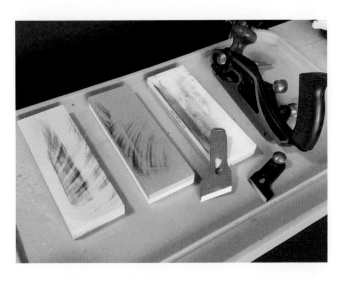

A skewed blade can be a challenge to sharpen using traditional honing guides.

Apply even pressure across the bevel as you sharpen a skewed plane iron.

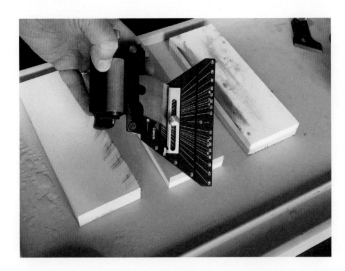

This attachment for the honing guide allows you to clamp a skewed blade at the proper bevel angle for sharpening.

Freehand sharpening a skewed iron means concentrating on keeping the bevel flat on the stone. As long as this is true, you don't need to be concerned with the skew angle – it takes care of itself.

Router plane

A router plane is another one of those tools that comes in handy for joinery applications, especially if you enjoy working with hand tools. There are a variety of blades you can purchase for them. Their primary function is to create a surface at a prescribed depth, such as a groove.

Whether you have picked up an old, antique router plane or purchased a new one, it's a good idea to make sure the back of the blade, opposite the bevel, is flat. Remember our rule: two flat surfaces intersect to create a sharp edge.

The back of the blade should be smooth all the way to the cutting edge.

Sharpening the bevel of a router plane blade can require a little thought. You need to set the bevel flat on the stone, but the shaft of the blade gets in the

While you can make or buy jigs that help with sharpening blades for router planes, it's just as easy to sharpen them by hand.

Flattening the back of the router plane blade is the first step to sharpness.

way. An easy solution is to move the sharpening stone parallel and near the edge of the workbench. Another solution is to elevate the stone to provide clearance for the shaft.

Keeping your hand planes sharp and ready to go to work at a moment's notice makes working in the shop much more enjoyable. And when you notice they aren't performing as they should, with the knowledge you have now, you can quickly touch up the irons and get right back to work.

Once the back of the router plane blade is flat, you won't have to do it again. Now you can turn your attention to the bevel.

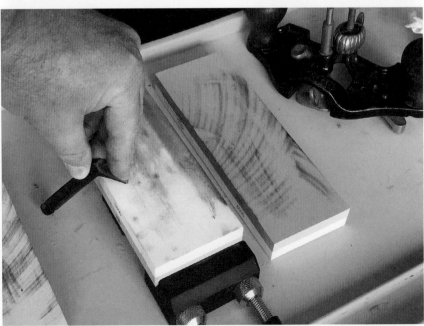

Sharpen the bevel as you would any other tool. The bevel's wide surface helps to register it flat on the stone.

2:3
Card scrapers

A scraper is a handy tool to have in the woodworking shop. Properly sharpened, it can smooth a wood surface better than sandpaper. Scraper planes, cabinet scrapers and card scrapers are especially useful for woods with wild grain patterns.

A scraper can create a silky-smooth surface without tearing out the grain. Scrapers are also handy for removing machining marks left by saws, planers and thicknessers.

A properly sharpened card scraper removes thin shavings of wood for a smooth surface.

Forming a burr

Scraper blades and card scrapers utilize a relatively thin steel blade. A burr is purposely formed along the cutting edge. It is the burr that does all the work of removing a thin shaving.

To improve the cutting action of a scraper plane or rectangular card scraper, the blade is flexed, or bowed, in the middle during use. This creates a cutting edge that is slightly arched so that it removes the most material in the centre while tapering off to no shaving at the edges. When using a card scraper by hand, the thumbs flex the blade. On a scraper plane or cabinet scraper, a screw mechanism slightly bows the blade.

Card scrapers come in a variety of shapes and sizes. Thinner scrapers can be bowed to a tighter radius to smooth smaller areas than their thicker counterparts.

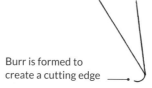

Burr is formed to create a cutting edge

Forming a burr along the cutting edge of a scraper blade or card scraper is the secret to getting thin shavings.

A scraper plane behaves like a smoothing plane, but is designed to scrape the surface to smooth hard-to-plane workpieces.

Card scrapers are available in a variety of shapes and sizes. Curved scrapers excel at smoothing moulding profiles such as crown or cove moulding.

Sharpening a scraper

The supplies you will need to sharpen a card scraper or scraper blade include a machinist's file for straight scrapers, a small diamond file for curved scrapers, a hardened steel burnishing rod, and a sharpening stone. Before sharpening a card scraper, I use a sharpening stone to remove any burr. You'll be forming a new burr so you need to start with square edges.

The next step smooths the edge in preparation for forming new burrs. To do this on a card scraper, I clamp the scraper in a wood vice and then use the file to smooth the edge. When the entire edge is shiny, you are ready to proceed to the next step.

It might take a little practice to hold the file square along the edge as you are filing. If you struggle with this, you can use the trick shown below. Once the edge is filed square, I like to polish it on a sharpening stone (1000-grit). This helps ensure that the resulting burr is as sharp as it can be.

Now you are ready to create the burrs. To do this, clamp the scraper in a vice. Use a hardened steel burnisher for this next step. You can find burnishers from many online woodworking supply retailers. In a pinch, I've sometimes used a round-shaft screwdriver.

Burnishing a scraper is not as difficult as it might appear. It involves applying moderate pressure on the burnisher, then pushing and pulling it across the edge of the scraper. You don't need to rotate the burnisher – just slide it across the edge, making sure to burnish the entire length of the scraper.

This first step starts to deform the steel at the outside corners of the scraper's edge. To create the final burr, there is a little more burnishing to do.

Use a file to create a smooth, square edge on the card scraper. Notice that I'm using my index fingers against the scraper to help hold the file square to the faces.

Clamp the file in the vice and use the worktop as a guide to file the edge of the card scraper smooth and square.

Start tilting the burnisher ever so slightly by lifting one end. You're now going to concentrate on the outside corner. As you tilt the burnisher, keep applying moderate pressure downward along the entire edge. Keep the burnisher moving as you make several strokes. Continue to angle the burnisher to about 10–15°. This angle creates the final burr. You should be able to feel the burr with your fingernail.

Repeat the process on the opposite face of the scraper. You will end up with two burrs – one on each side of the scraper. You can go ahead and flip the scraper over to create burrs on the opposite edge, but you'll need to protect the burrs you have just completed.

To sharpen a curved scraper, the same process applies. Since you can't polish the curved edge on a sharpening stone, I like to use a small diamond file.

Using a burnisher on a curved scraper is easier than it might seem: just remember to keep applying pressure to the edge as you go.

There's one thing I want to point out. For small scrapers that may be hard to burnish to form a hook, you can get perfectly acceptable results by forming a sharp corner along the scraper edges. You do this by honing with a sharpening stone and diamond file. A sharp, square edge makes for an effective scraper. In fact, many craftspeople in centuries gone by would use pieces of broken glass as scrapers.

Place the scraper face on the sharpening stone and file away the old burr. Do this for all the edges on both sides of the scraper.

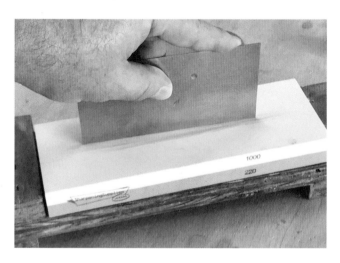

Holding the scraper square to the stone, polish the edge until the scratches left by the file are gone.

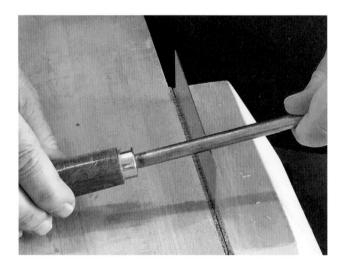

Angle the burnisher to about 10–15° to form the final burr along the edge.

A burnisher deforms the steel at the edges of the card scraper to begin forming a burr. Start with the burnisher square to the faces of the scraper.

Sharpening the blades for a scraper plane or cabinet scraper is no more difficult than what I've explained so far. The process is very similar; the only thing that is different is that there is a 45° bevel along the cutting edge. When you're filing, you will want to maintain that same angle.

When you form the burr, start with the burnisher following the angle of the bevel, then tilt the burnisher slightly to form the cutting burr on the opposite face of the blade from the bevel.

It doesn't take much of an angle to create the burr. You can actually curl the burr over too far, which makes it difficult to engage the wood for cutting.

Sharpening and using a scraper takes practice. Adjustments in the angle of the scraper against the wood are often needed until you feel the burr start to cut. This is common. If you're having to angle the scraper excessively, it is likely you've gone too far when burnishing.

As you are using a scraper, the friction from the cutting action will heat up the blade. It doesn't take long before the burr is worn and is not cutting as effectively. For card scrapers, simply switch to a fresh edge. When all the edges lose their cutting ability, it is time to resharpen them. Once you learn the process, it doesn't take long.

A small diamond file is ideal for polishing the edge of a curved scraper before using a burnisher to form the burr.

Burnish the edges of a curved scraper the same way you would a straight scraper edge.

The burr on a cabinet scraper blade is formed on the face opposite the bevel. Start by burnishing at the same angle as the bevel, then gradually tilt the burnisher a few degrees to create the burr.

To sharpen a blade for a cabinet scraper, start by polishing the bevel first with a file and then on a sharpening stone.

2:4
Carving tools

If you spend any time with woodcarvers, you'll soon gain a whole new appreciation for sharp tools. Carvers are fanatics about sharpness. They have to be. All their tools are expected to make clean cuts in wood regardless of the grain direction. The resulting surface is crisp and free of tearout.

Carving tools fall into four broad categories: chisels, gouges, V-parting tools and knives. As you might expect, chisels have a straight cutting edge. Carving chisels may have a single or double bevel. Sharpening a carving chisel is similar to sharpening a standard woodworking bench chisel.

Woodcarving is the surest test of the sharpness of your carving tools.

The range of carving tools

Gouges have U-shaped cutting edges and vary in width and radius, or sweep. The most common types of gouges are made with the bevel on the outside of the sweep. These are referred to as out-cannel gouges. In-cannel gouges are made with the bevel on the inside of the sweep. Gouges offer some unique challenges in sharpening in order to maintain the proper shape.

V-parting tools, as the name suggests, feature V-shaped cutting edges. The angle of the 'V' can vary. For the purposes of sharpening, you can treat the bevel on each side of the 'V' as a separate chisel.

Carving knives generally feature short blades that can be straight or curved. You would sharpen these as you might a conventional knife.

There's one thing I need to point out. Each woodcarver has their own preference for the shape and configuration of the cutting edge and bevel on their carving tools. It is not uncommon for a carver to regrind a tool to suit their needs. In this chapter, we will focus on sharpening and honing the cutting edge, regardless of shape.

Most carvers are all about honing and stropping the edge of their tools frequently while they work. Serious carvers use powered equipment to do this. We'll talk about a couple of the options you can use to keep your carving tools scary sharp.

The hobbyist carver may choose to use sharpening stones and strops. It may take more time to do this by hand versus using a powered tool, but the results are no less satisfactory. Regardless of how you decide to sharpen carving tools, one thing to remember is to always pull the tool away from the cutting edge on the sharpening medium.

Carving knives come in a variety of blade configurations.

Gouges

The challenge with sharpening a gouge is maintaining a consistent edge throughout the sweep. This is a little easier on out-cannel gouges since the bevel is on the outside of the blade. The main thing to remember is to keep the tool rotating as it is in contact with the sharpening medium.

The important thing to watch for is maintaining the same bevel angle. This isn't as critical as it might be on other tools, but you'll get a more uniform cutting edge if you pay attention to this detail.

Rolling the gouge from side to side as you move the gouge towards you is one of the keys to getting a smooth edge.

Using a sharpening stone, start with the gouge rolled to the outside corner.

Finish up with the sweep on the opposite corner as you finish pulling the gouge across the sharpening stone.

This method is a quick and easy way to touch up the edge as you work. If the edge or bevel needs to be reshaped, use a coarse stone and follow the same technique. Then you can work your way up through finer grits to a more polished edge.

One tool you can use to refine the edge of a gouge is a slipstone. Slipstones come in a variety of shapes to address curved or unique edge profiles.

When using a slipstone, the same rule applies – remember to always pull the gouge away from the cutting edge. After using a sharpening stone or slipstone, you will want to strop the edge to a polish. This is a sure way to get the sharpest edge possible.

To remove any burr on the inside edge of a gouge, or when honing an in-cannel gouge, with the bevel on the inside of the sweep, you can use a slipstone here as well. You can hone gouges using a small piece of wet/dry sandpaper or lapping film wrapped around a pencil or dowel. This makes it easy to hone the inside radius of any gouge.

A trick you can use to hone the edge of an out-cannel gouge is to use a piece of scrap wood

As you pull the gouge towards you, start to roll the cutting edge to the opposite side while maintaining the same bevel angle.

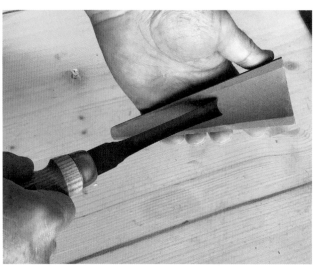

A curved slipstone can help sharpen the edge of a gouge.

A slipstone with a convex edge can remove the burr on out-cannel gouges or hone the bevel on an in-cannel gouge.

and honing compound. You use the gouge to carve out a trough in the wood. Then apply honing compound to the trough. Because you used the gouge to make the trough, its profile is guaranteed to match the cutting edge of the tool.

Draw the tool back through the trough in the direction away from the cutting edge. Make several passes to put a polish on the edge. You can test the sharpness of the tool by cutting into the wood. The result should be a clean cut with no tearout or chipping.

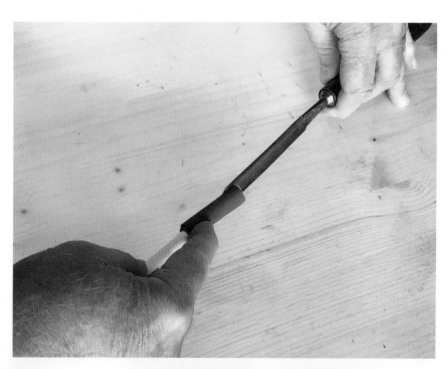

You can get creative when honing tools. Here, I'm using sandpaper wrapped around a pencil to touch up the inside edge of this carving gouge.

Apply honing compound to a trough carved into the wood using the tool you want to hone.

Make test cuts to check your progress when honing.

V-tools

Sharpening a V-tool is almost like sharpening a pair of straight chisels. You can touch up the bevels easily on a sharpening stone.

After you hone one side of the V-tool, rotate it 90° and repeat the process. Remember to always pull away from the cutting edge. Lift the tool before repositioning it at the opposite end of the stone to make subsequent strokes.

The point of the 'V' on parting tools has a small radius. You can carefully rotate the tool on the point as you pull it across the stone. A slipstone comes in handy to remove any burrs on the inside edge.

Lay the bevel of the V-tool flat on the stone and draw it towards you, making several strokes.

A slipstone with a sharp edge can get into tight corners.

Carving knives

You can treat a carving knife almost like any other knife when it comes to sharpening – it just requires more frequent honing during use.

I use a sharpening stone to keep the cutting edge nice and straight. A coarse stone can quickly remove small nicks in the edge to restore it.

You can work your way through finer grits until you see a polished edge. The next step would be to use a strop. This creates the final, razor-sharp edge.

Leather is not an absolute requirement as a honing material; you can make a hone from almost any material. Popular options are hardwood scraps or pieces of MDF (medium-density fibreboard). You can shape the hardwood or MDF to conform to the shape of the tool, apply honing compound, and you're in business.

After honing, the test I use for sharpness is to make a cut across the end grain of a soft wood. If it slices the wood fibres cleanly instead of crushing them, your knife is ready to be put to work.

Try to match the knife's original bevel angle and push or pull the blade away from the cutting edge.

Make several passes on a leather strop charged with a honing compound. Hone both sides of the knife equally.

Powered honing machines

A busy carver will need to touch up the edge of their carving tools quite often. A quick honing is usually all that is needed. A lot of carvers will use powered devices simply for their speed and efficiency.

A common accessory that carvers use for powered honing is a felt or cloth wheel. The soft wheels, when charged with a honing compound, conform to the shape of the tool and create a mirror polish. You can purchase these wheels in a variety of sizes. Some include arbors that you can chuck into a drill press.

When using a soft wheel, it is important to orientate the cutting edge of the tool in the same direction as the rotation of the wheel. In other words, the wheel should be moving away from the cutting edge. Otherwise, the cutting edge can dig into the wheel, sending the tool flying out of your hands. A little caution and awareness is in order.

You can purchase this style of wheel to fit a bench grinder, as shown below. Just a couple of seconds with the tool contacting the wheel can restore the cutting edge. The soft texture of the

Cloth or felt wheels are an inexpensive option for keeping carving tools as sharp as they can be.

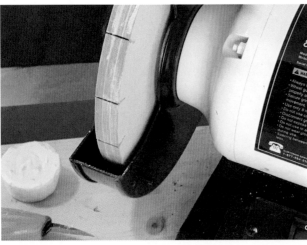

The firmer texture of this paper wheel is especially suited for knives, but can also be used for most other carving tools.

Notice the orientation of the tool to the downward spinning direction of the cloth wheel mounted on this bench grinder.

wheel wraps around the shape of the tool's edge for uniform honing. One manufacturer makes honing wheels for bench grinders from glued-up layers of paper. These firmer wheels can be charged with an abrasive compound to put an edge on most tools.

The other option for honing that seems to be popular among carvers and woodworkers is the low-speed machine shown below. It uses abrasives adhered to a glass or slotted plastic wheel. For honing, I like to start with 3600- or 6000-grit sandpaper on the glass wheel.

This company also makes a felt wheel and leather hone for the unit. The felt wheel provides a softer surface that conforms more to the shape of the tool.

The leather hone comes attached to a glass wheel, which ensures flatness. Many carvers use the leather hone exclusively to keep their tools razor sharp during a project.

Keeping your carving tools sharp is the key to success and great-looking results. You can choose the sharpening and honing options that suit your budget and needs. Once you recognize the benefits of frequent honing, you'll have a new appreciation for sharp tools.

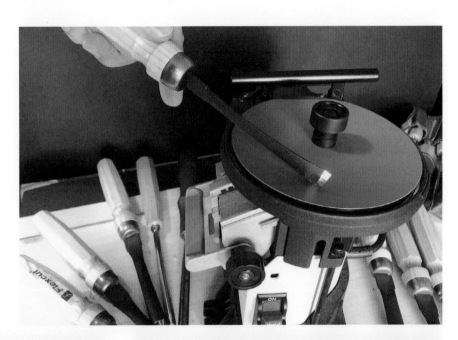

The Work Sharp equipped with a low-speed wheel and fine-grit abrasive makes quick work of honing an edge.

Before using the felt wheel, apply a honing compound to the surface.

After applying honing compound to the leather hone, it quickly creates a mirror polish and sharp cutting edge.

2:5
Garden tools

When you think of sharpening tools, lawn and garden tools may not come to mind immediately. But if you have ever used a dull set of pruners, you can appreciate how sharp tools can make a difference in your gardening and landscaping tasks.

Even garden tools such as shovels, cultivators and hoes can benefit from having a sharper edge. This helps them cut into tough soil and sever small roots. Compared to fine-edged tools like chisels and kitchen knives, these hardworking tools don't require a razor-sharp edge. But any work you can do to create more of a bevelled cutting edge will only make using the tool easier with less effort.

Sharpening supplies for garden tools don't need to be extensive or expensive. Some garden centres sell inexpensive, rough stones that are used for sharpening. They do a great job on the edges of soil-cutting tools like shovels and hoes. You can also use a standard flat metalworking file available wherever tools are sold.

Keeping the cutting edges of your lawn and garden tools sharp makes outdoor chores more relaxing.

Digging tools

Any tool that needs to cut through sod or tough clay soil can benefit from a little sharpening. Most inexpensive shovel blades are stamped from steel at the factory, leaving a blunt, square edge. With a little work, you can form a slight bevel along the cutting edge. You'll then find that your digging tasks require a little less effort.

To create the bevelled edge, start with the file or stone placed on the edge of the tool, starting at the tip of the file. As you push the file forward, make a sweeping motion along the edge to start forming a bevel. Repeat this filing and sweeping motion along the entire edge of the tool. The edge does not need to be razor thin. Creating an edge that is too sharp will dull quickly during use. You just need to file off the sharp corner to form a slight bevel.

On tools that have had a bevel ground at the factory, simply follow the existing bevel angle to refine the edge. With regular sharpening, you'll find that it takes only a few strokes to touch it up.

A metal or coarse diamond file works well to create a bevelled cutting edge on a shovel.

Weeding and cultivating tools

Just like a shovel, tools used for weeding and cultivating soil can benefit from a little sharpening. Again, creating a stout cutting edge is the key. This makes it easier for the tool to cut through tough weeds and roots or break up lumps of soil.

The process is the same as before. Make long, sweeping strokes across the edge, following the existing bevel angle. Don't worry about removing all the nicks and dings – the goal is to file away the rough spots and make the edge more suitable for digging.

A coarse diamond file may be all you need to sharpen the edge of a cultivating or weeding tool.

Garden trowel

Since garden trowels are also used for digging and creating holes for plants or seeds, you can treat a trowel like a miniature shovel. Use a file to create or refine a bevel along the edges of the trowel. For trowels that have been stamped from steel, it will take a little work to form the initial bevel. After that, a touch-up with a stone or file on a regular basis will keep the trowel in great shape for your gardening tasks.

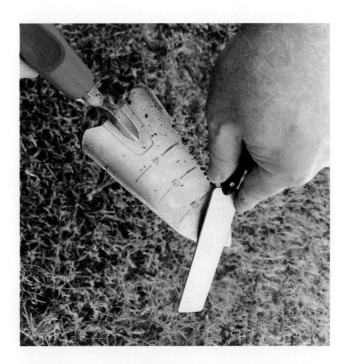

A coarse stone or diamond file makes quick work of refining the edges of a trowel for easier digging.

Pruners

There are two styles of pruners: anvil pruners and bypass pruners. Anvil pruners feature a stiff cutting blade that forces the plant stem against a flat plate – or anvil – on the opposing jaw. This style of pruner is designed for cutting hard, woody material. These pruners are easily sharpened by touching up the bevels on the cutting blade.

Bypass pruners, on the other hand, work more like a pair of shears or scissors. The cutting action happens as the blades rub against each other when forcing them closed. One or both blades can have a bevelled cutting edge that must be sharp to do an effective job at making clean cuts in plant material. Sharpening bypass pruners involves touching up two

A tapered diamond file has a flat side suitable for ensuring the back of the cutting blade is flat. For bypass shears, it is best to also smooth the back of each blade.

Use long, even strokes across the face of the bevel until the cutting edge becomes sharp.

surfaces: the bevel and the 'back' or flat side of the blade. Again, the goal is not to remove all the nicks; it is more important to make sure that the back and bevel are relatively flat and meet at a sharp edge.

For these tasks I like to use a metalworking file, diamond file or small diamond sharpening stone. I usually start by making sure the back, or flat area, of each blade is smooth, especially at the cutting edge.

Once the back of each blade is flat, you can turn your attention to the bevelled edge. Use long, sweeping strokes along the length of the bevel while paying attention to keep the file at the same angle as the bevel. It might seem difficult at first, but you will soon get a feel for it and it will become second nature.

After you have completed the above steps, make some test cuts on plant material. The pruners should slice cleanly through the stems without tearing. In some cases, you may need to adjust the tension on the bolt that connects the two blades. The cutting edges of the two blades should be in contact with one another throughout the entire stroke of opening and closing the blades.

Garden shears

Garden shears are more scissor-like than any other garden tool. The bevelled cutting edge of each blade works together to sever plant fibres for a clean cut. If garden shears are dull, they will do more tearing than cutting, leaving a ragged cut.

I sharpen shears in much the same fashion as bypass pruners. I start by rubbing a file or stone across the back to eliminate high spots from nicks or dings to the cutting edge. Then you can turn your attention to the bevelled edges. The goal is to touch up the bevel until the cutting edge is sharp.

Touching up the edges of your garden tools is good practice. Keeping them sharp and ready to go makes your time in the garden more enjoyable.

Touch up the cutting edge of garden shears with a small file. It is also a good idea to ensure the back of each blade is flat.

2:6
Kitchen tools

Cutlery is the unsung hero of the kitchen. We rely on knives to prepare food for our meals. Unfortunately, knife edges get dull before we know it, scissors stop making clean cuts and vegetable peelers get dinged up in the drawer. Fortunately, with a little care and attention, you can restore the cutting edges in just a few minutes.

Besides your standard set of kitchen knives, anything with a cutting edge is fair game for sharpening. Serrated bread knives, pizza cutters, scissors and vegetable peelers can all benefit from a quick honing. The modest investment in time is well worth the effort when it comes time to use the tool. I often hear the exclamation, 'Wow! I didn't know this could be so sharp!'

Periodic sharpening will keep your knives and other cutting tools in tip-top shape ready for action.

Investing a few minutes of time sharpening kitchen utensils makes a big difference when it's your turn to play chef.

Care and use of knives

When it comes to purchasing knives, I always advise buying the best quality you can afford. Doing so ensures that you're getting a knife made from steel that can be sharpened easily and will last for decades. Inexpensive knives tend to be made from stainless steel, which can be difficult to sharpen and won't hold an edge as well as a better-quality knife.

Always use a cutting board or mat when using a knife for slicing, dicing and chopping foods. The ideal cutting board is made from end-grain hardwood such as maple, reminiscent of chopping blocks found in a butcher shop. The wood fibres help absorb the impact of the cutting edge. Plastic boards and mats are a suitable alternative. Avoid using knives on hard plastic, porcelain, ceramic or china plates – the hard surfaces will dull keen edges quickly.

Another thing that will help ensure that your knives stay sharper longer is to clean them by hand.

Avoid putting them in the automatic dishwasher. If the knife has a wood handle, the wood can't tolerate the cycles of high heat, humidity and drying in a dishwasher. This causes the wood to dry out and crack. Also, knives in the dishwasher can get knocked around by the action of the spray arms. If the knives bang against other utensils and dishes, the cutting edge can become nicked or damaged.

Properly storing the knives will greatly add to the life of the cutting edge before it needs to be sharpened. Use a wood knife block or other method to keep the knife blade from contacting other knives or metal objects. If you store your knives in a drawer, keep them in a knife storage rack to avoid damaging the blade.

Whenever you sharpen utensils that are used for food preparation, be sure to give them a good wash with washing-up liquid and water before using them. This removes any metal particles and lubricant.

A rack like this one keeps knives separated to protect the cutting edges while making them visible for quick and easy selection of the appropriate knife for the task.

Wall-mounted knife racks save worktop space and make the knives easily accessible.

A traditional knife block does a great job of protecting the fragile cutting edges but makes it more difficult to quickly select the desired knife since its blade is hidden in the block.

This drawer rack for kitchen knives keeps the knives secure and separated to protect the cutting edges.

Knife sharpening

There are dozens of tools and methods for sharpening knives, ranging from a simple honing stone to more complex jigs and machines. I'll show you a few ways I like to sharpen knives, but the tools and methods you use will depend on your budget and comfort level.

Sharpening steel

If you've watched many cooking shows, you may have seen a chef use a sharpening steel. In its simplest form, it's a smooth steel rod with a handle. You may also see them with small ridges running down the length of the rod. Many chefs use a

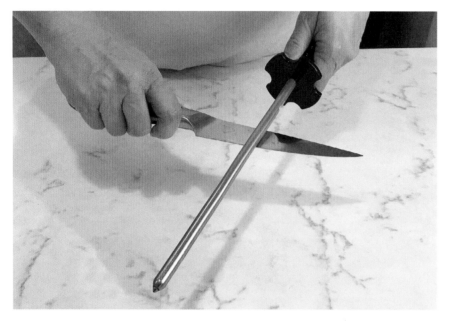

Holding the steel away from your body is a safe method to use if you're just learning.

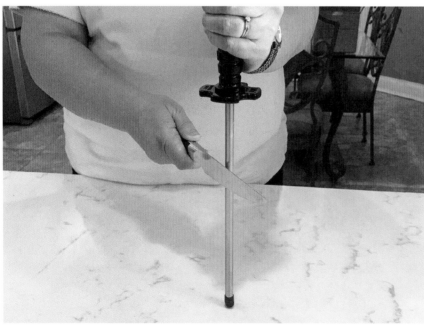

Resting the sharpening steel vertically on the worktop makes it easy to master the proper technique of honing a knife.

sharpening steel to hone the edges of their knives before putting them to use.

In truth, a sharpening steel was not designed to sharpen at all. As a blade gets dull from use and the chopping action on a cutting board, the metal on the blade deforms slightly. The purpose of the steel is to force the metal back into position to realign the cutting edge. Traditional steels don't remove any metal. You would have to use a sharpening stone or mechanical sharpener to remove metal to form a clean, new cutting edge.

To eliminate the extra step of sharpening, steels have evolved to include fine diamond abrasive particles bonded to the steel rod. This abrasive removes metal while realigning the cutting edge. This dual-purpose steel sharpens the edge and straightens it at the same time.

To use a sharpening steel, you can hold it a few different ways. You'll often see professionals hold the steel with rod pointing up and away from their body. They will have the cutting edge of the knife facing towards the handle end of the sharpening steel.

Another method of holding the steel – and one that's easier to master – is to position the rod vertically with the end resting on the worktop.

To touch up the cutting edge on a sharpening steel, start by setting the edge of the knife against the steel rod. Now, angle the top of the blade away from the rod to the approximate bevel angle of the cutting edge. With the heel (handle end) of the knife at the handle end of the sharpening steel, slice down the rod as you pull the knife back towards you. Try to make this one sweeping motion while maintaining the angle of the blade against the rod. The slicing motion is like paring the skin or peel from a piece of fruit or vegetable.

Place the knife on the opposite edge of the rod and repeat the process to hone the other edge.

Alternate back and forth to maintain even sharpening on both sides. As you gain experience, you'll get faster and it will become second nature. Eight to ten strokes on each side should be enough to restore the cutting edge. If it takes more than that, you may need to use sharpening stones or a mechanical sharpener to restore the edge before honing.

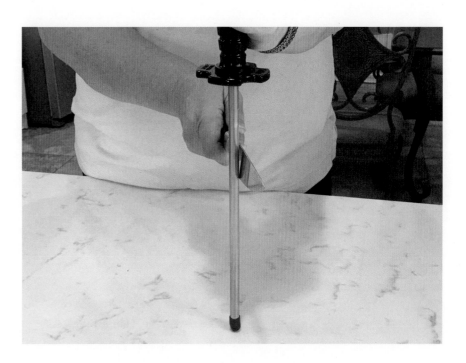

Use the same number of strokes on each side of the sharpening steel, being careful to maintain the same angle.

Knife sharpeners

When a knife edge cannot be recovered by honing alone, it is time to go to something a little more aggressive. Commercial knife-sharpening devices range from the very inexpensive to high-end, more expensive systems.

The simplest type of knife sharpener consists of a plastic handle that holds two carbide blades. The blades are oriented at an angle to form a 'V' that sharpens both sides of the knife blade at the same time. To use this type of sharpener, position the knife in the notch with the heel of the blade engaged. Then, with moderate pressure, pull the knife towards you in one smooth, even stroke along the entire length of the blade. Repeat this a few times, then visually inspect the edge to ensure even sharpening progress.

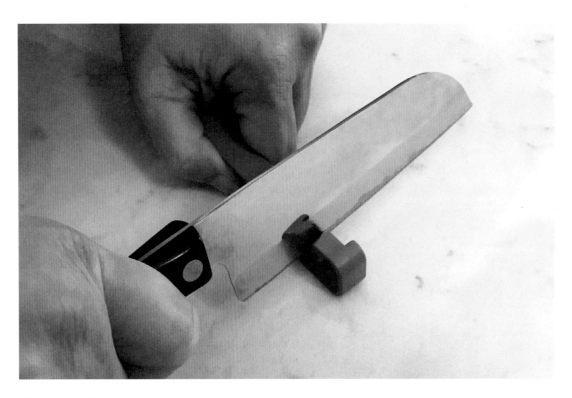

This simple and inexpensive sharpener can help restore an edge before final honing.

Using sharpening stones

I believe that every kitchen should have a set of sharpening stones handy. They are a modest investment useful for a variety of sharpening tasks. The type of stones you purchase will depend on your budget and desired features (see pages 34–41).

When using a larger sharpening stone, it is helpful to use a holder for the stone to keep it from sliding around on your worktop. Since most stones require a lubricant, you will also want to protect the worktop. For this, you can use an old baking tray, serving tray or a stack of newspapers. I often use a silicone mat that serves two purposes: it protects the worktop and provides a non-slip surface for the stone.

When using sharpening stones, be sure to follow the manufacturer's recommendations for use, care and choosing the proper lubricant.

A silicone mat is ideal for sharpening tasks. Its non-slip surface also protects the worktop.

Tip

Here's a tip I learned to use if I run across a dull knife and lack any tools for sharpening: use a ceramic coffee mug. If you turn most mugs or cups upside down, you'll discover that the rim of the base is unglazed. This provides a slightly abrasive surface that you can use in a pinch to touch up the edge of a knife. Hold the knife edge against the ceramic at an angle that matches the bevel angle on the knife. Draw the knife across the ceramic, making the same number of strokes on each side of the blade.

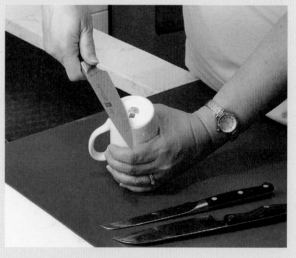

Use the unglazed portion of a ceramic cup as a honing stone for your knives.

Waterstones will require access to water. I have a spray bottle nearby to keep the stone wet while I'm sharpening. Some waterstones require soaking in water before you sharpen. Other stones might be damaged by soaking, so following the instructions that came with the stones is a good idea for protecting your investment.

Diamond stones can be used dry, but will perform better when used with a lubricant. You can use a special lubricant designed for the type of stone, or mix a few drops of washing-up liquid in a spray bottle with water. The lubricants help keep the 'swarf', or dust, generated during the sharpening process from clogging the stone.

The technique for sharpening knives using sharpening stones is easy to master with a little practice. As a guideline, coarse stones are generally used to restore badly damaged cutting edges. Finer stones are used for honing and polishing. Always start with the coarsest stone you think you'll need to restore the edge. Then work up through successively finer grits until you get a polished, razor-sharp edge.

It is important to sharpen both sides of the knife evenly. This helps maintain the straight cutting edge. Serrated knives and knives with a bevelled edge on one side only are the exception that we'll talk about later.

Start with the tip of the knife engaged on the stone. Angle the back of the knife up away from the stone to match the bevel angle on the cutting edge.

The easiest way I have found to sharpen a knife on a stone is to use long, even strokes along the length of the cutting edge, starting at the tip. Maintain an angle that keeps the bevelled edge tight against the stone.

While applying moderate pressure to the blade where it contacts the stone, move the knife lengthwise along the blade and away from you at the same time using an arcing motion. The idea is to use as much of the surface of the stone as possible for even wear.

Sharpen up through at least 1200-grit. Finer grits have the benefit of removing the fine scratches and creating a polished edge that will be the ultimate in sharpness.

My test for sharpness in the kitchen is how easily the knife can cut thin slices of tomato. The knife should cut through the skin of the tomato with little effort. If it requires a 'sawing' motion, it's time to go back to the stones and hone the edge.

Slide the knife across the stone in one even stroke along the cutting edge. It is important to maintain the same angle of contact with the stone as you do this.

Serrated knives

Looking at a serrated knife, you may scratch your head wondering if and how it can be sharpened. If you study the knife edge closely, you'll see a series of notches, or gullets, that have been ground on one side of the blade. These form the serrations and make the knife easier to cut bread, thick-skinned vegetables and fruits such as melons and tomatoes, or cooked meats. The shape of each serration forms two pointed edges that act like the teeth of a saw. They multiply the cutting action of the knife's edge.

In the photo below, you can see the serrations on two knives. The upper knife is one that has seen years of abuse without any attempt at sharpening. You can see the points are worn, bent or missing. Even some of the gullet areas have been damaged.

The lower knife is a newer serrated knife that has been well cared for. The points of the serrations form an even line along the cutting edge and remain sharp. The gullets are well defined and smooth.

Sharpening a serrated knife boils down to thinking of each serration, or gullet, as a curved bevel that forms a rounded cutting edge. With that in mind, the first thing to do is flatten the opposite side of the knife to remove burrs and create a reference surface for a sharp cutting edge.

To sharpen the serrated edge of the knife, you'll need a sharpening stone that has a small radius to fit the curved bevel of the gullet. You can use a short length of small-diameter wood dowel wrapped with a small piece of wet/dry sandpaper. A common tool for sharpening and honing curved surfaces is a slipstone. Slipstones can vary in shape; the most common version looks like a thin wedge when viewed from the end. Each long edge of the slipstone is formed with a small radius. You can also purchase special devices specifically designed for sharpening serrated knives.

The process of sharpening a serrated knife takes a little time because of all of the curved, bevelled surfaces, but once you get started, it becomes routine.

Start by setting the stone in the gullet and finding the bevel angle. Make long strokes towards the cutting edge while working side to side in the gullet. When the entire gullet has been touched up, move onto the next one. Finally, remove any burrs on the back side of the knife by setting it flat on a fine sharpening stone and making a few strokes, checking that all the burrs have been removed.

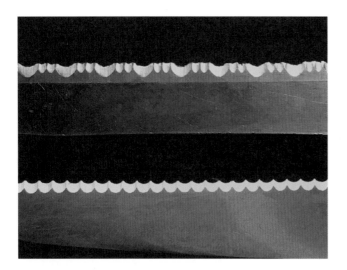

The upper serrated knife has been neglected and shows significant damage to the cutting edges of the serrations. The lower knife shows well-defined serrations with sharp points and smooth gullets.

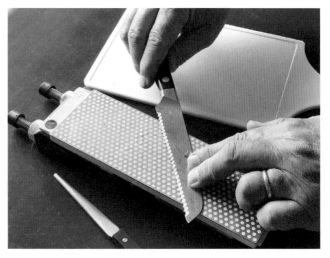

Flatten and polish the back of the knife before focusing your attention on the gullets of the serrations.

Ceramic knives

Technology has brought about the manufacture of ceramic knives. They have the advantages of maintaining a sharp edge for a long time and are rustproof. They are a little fragile, so it pays to handle them with care and store them to protect them from damage.

Because of the ceramic material, you cannot use traditional waterstones or oil stones to sharpen them – the ceramic is harder than the stones. The only material suitable for sharpening ceramic knives is diamond. Therefore, if you own ceramic knives, it is a good idea to have a few small diamond stones on hand.

The process of sharpening is no different than sharpening a steel knife. Use a lubricant on the stone and make long, sweeping strokes along the length of the blade. Try to maintain the original bevel angle as you sharpen.

A slipstone makes a great tool for sharpening a serrated knife.

This sharpening device uses a triangular-shaped stone that makes it easy to touch up the edges of a serrated knife.

Sharpen a ceramic knife using a diamond stone with the same technique as sharpening a steel knife.

Advanced sharpening options

As I mentioned earlier, there are several options for reliably and easily sharpening knives in the kitchen. One such device uses small diamond-coated abrasive plates. The plates are essentially miniature sharpening stones. Like the simple jig shown below, the plates are oriented in a 'V' shape to sharpen both sides of the knife simultaneously. The plates are spring-loaded to apply pressure to the blade during the sharpening operation.

To use this style of sharpener, place the knife in the slot until it bottoms out. This action forces the spring-loaded diamond stones apart as they stay snug against the blade. With the blade all the way forward, pull the blade back towards you and out of the device. Repeat the process several times. Blades that are dull will require more strokes to restore the cutting edge.

If you hire a professional to sharpen your knives, chances are they would use an abrasive belt on a machine. The belts range in grits from coarse, for rough shaping and removal of nicks, to finer polishing belts for final honing. You can use the same basic process at home with the machine shown below. It is designed for home use and the do-it-yourselfer. Out of the box, it uses small abrasive belts to restore an edge on a knife.

This sharpener features a guide slot on each side of the belt to make sharpening both sides of a knife a foolproof operation.

If the knife has been neglected for some time and is damaged or dull, you will want to start with a coarse belt. Once the edge has been reshaped, you can work your way up through finer grits until the edge is polished. Don't be tempted to skip grits: the goal is to remove the scratches left by the previous grit so that you end up with a mirror polish. With a powered device driving the belt, the process is quite quick.

On this device, there is a tool rest that is at the proper angle for sharpening the bevel on scissors. To do this, rest the flat (back) of the blade on the tool

This sharpener features a deep slot that keeps the knife blade vertical as you pass it between the spring-loaded diamond plates.

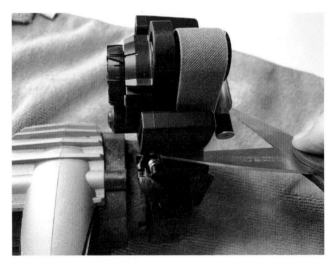

Using a powered belt sharpener is a quick and easy way to restore dull scissors and shears.

rest and move the blade across the belt in a smooth, continuous motion. When using a powered belt sharpener, be aware that they generate a lot of fine dust, so I recommend sharpening the knives outdoors or in a garage.

This sharpening device is also available with a blade-grinding attachment that steps up the features and options for sharpening knives. It is geared towards the serious user who wants the ultimate in flexibility.

Freehand sharpening using this set-up is not as scary as it might seem; it just takes a little practice. This device allows you to set the angle of the grinding face of the belt to accommodate a variety of bevel angles. The trick is in learning how to hold the knife blade parallel to the worktop.

This set-up works particularly well for knives with curved blades and smaller knives. It provides more clearance to allow the entire length of the blade to contact the belt without interference.

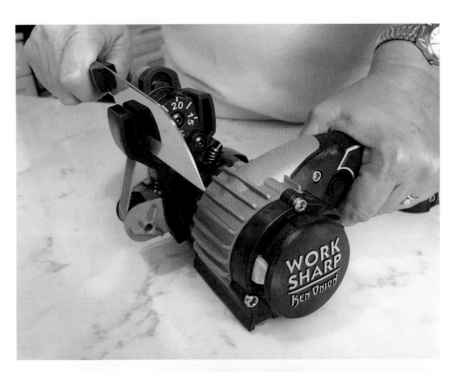

This sharpener features an adjustable guide for the bevel angle. Abrasive belts make quick work of restoring the knife's edge.

The blade-grinding attachment uses wider belts and provides easy access for sharpening a blade freehand.

Sharpening other kitchen gadgets

Almost anything in the kitchen with a cutting edge can be sharpened. This includes pizza cutters and vegetable peelers. You just need to find the proper sharpening tool that can address the bevels on the cutting edges.

To sharpen a wheeled pizza cutter, I find a small diamond stone or file ideal for dressing up the edge. Use one finger to hold the wheel stationary as you make strokes along the cutting edge, following the same bevel angle.

When storing a pizza wheel, treat it like a knife. If it has a cover, use it to protect the cutting edge. Otherwise, store it in a location and in a way that prevents accidental dings and damage.

Some vegetable peelers have dual cutting edges. This makes it easy to cut in either direction.

If it has a cutting edge, chances are you'll be able to sharpen it.

Use a diamond file or small stone to restore the cutting edge on a pizza wheel. Be sure to address both sides of the wheel. Don't worry about small nicks and dings; they won't affect the cutting ability.

Sharpening the bevels is best done with a small diamond stone or file – in fact, you can use a diamond nail file. Its size makes it ideal for getting into small areas.

The key is to keep the file flat on the bevel of the cutting edge. Long, even strokes across the edge yield the best results.

A small, dual-sided diamond file with a coarse grit on one side and finer grit on the other is a handy tool to have around for sharpening.

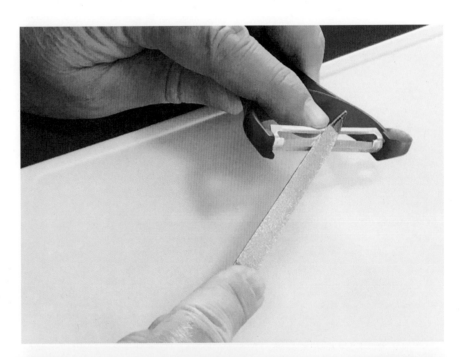

A diamond nail file can come to the rescue in a pinch. It is suitable for touching up the edges of small kitchen tools such as this vegetable peeler.

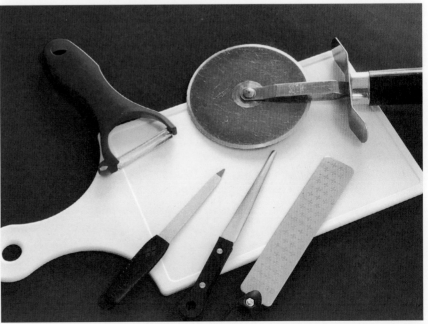

Diamond-coated tools make sharpening kitchen accessories an easy task.

2:7
Router bits

Most router bits feature carbide cutting edges and are a considerable investment. Carbide is formulated to withstand the high heat generated from friction when routing. When a router bit begins to get dull, it can cause burning and chatter marks, resulting in a rough surface on the wood that must be sanded.

Part of the problem may simply be that the router bit needs to be cleaned. Pitch and resin from the wood tend to build up along the cutting edges, reducing their effectiveness.

After a good cleaning, it takes very little time to touch up and hone the carbide. It's a simple operation that can pay off in big dividends in routing performance and life of the router bit.

Router bits can become dull just like any other tool. Fortunately, you can touch up the edges easily.

When is a router bit dull?

How do you recognize when a router bit is dull? When it starts to burn the wood or takes an extraordinary amount of effort to push the bit through the workpiece, it is time to take a look at the condition of the bit.

The first thing I look at is the carbide. If the carbide cutting edges are chipped or cracked, it is time to throw the bit away and buy a new one. Chipped carbide can eventually fracture during use and send metal particles flying.

The next thing I do is give the router bit a thorough cleaning. There are a variety of bit and blade cleaners available. You can also use a strong detergent. If the router bit has a bearing, remove the bearing first. Then soak the bit in the cleaning solution and use a nylon-bristle brush to remove dirt

sawdust and pitch from the wood. Sometimes all that is needed is a good cleaning to restore the bit to like-new performance.

If, after inspecting the cutting edges of the carbide, you determine that it would help to sharpen them, it's an easy process. Since we're dealing with carbide – a very hard metal – the most effective abrasive is diamond.

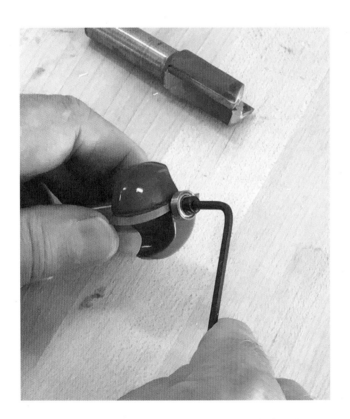

On bearing-guided router bits, remove the bearing before cleaning or sharpening the bit.

These small diamond stones are the perfect choice for sharpening router bits.

Sharpening a router bit

When sharpening a router bit, you'll be addressing the inside flat face of the carbide. It is important not to touch the outside edges or bevels of the bit because this can change the shape and diameter of the bit.

The process of sharpening a bit couldn't be simpler. Using a diamond hone, place the face of the carbide flat on the hone. The diamond hones I use are two-sided with 300-grit on one side and 600-grit on the other. Start with the 300-grit until you see a uniform scratch pattern on the carbide. Finish with the 600-grit side to remove the scratches left by the 300-grit.

Now all you need to do is install the bearing, washer and screw, making sure the screw is tight.

Sharpening a bit without a bearing follows the same procedure. First give the bit a good cleaning and inspect the carbide. Then use the diamond hone to touch up the carbide faces.

On straight router bits like the one shown in the left photo below, you can also use a small diamond file to touch up the ends of the carbide cutters. These edges are the first to engage the wood when making plunge cuts with your router. They're responsible for leaving a smooth bottom to dados, grooves and rabbets made with a router. Since touching up these edges doesn't affect the diameter of the bit, it is perfectly fine to give them a little attention.

Giving your router bits a little care and attention every once in a while can increase their lifespan and prolong your investment.

Polish inside face of carbide only

The inside face of the carbide cutter is the only area you need to give your attention to when sharpening a router bit.

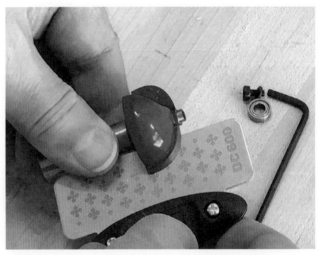

Use a small diamond hone to polish the inside face of the carbide cutters.

2:8

Planer/thicknesser blades

When it comes to milling wood to final thickness with square edges, a power planer/thicknesser is the go-to tool in the workshop. The planer's rotary cutting head contains a number of knives that remove shavings to create a smooth, flat surface and edge on your wood.

The thicknesser works in similar fashion to remove material to reduce the thickness of a workpiece and create a smooth face parallel to the original jointed face. The combination of a planer/thicknesser with properly sharpened knives is the first step to obtaining square and flat workpieces with a consistent thickness. This makes your project go together much more smoothly.

After milling hundreds of board feet of wood, it stands to reason that planer/thicknesser knives will eventually need to be resharpened or replaced. It's not difficult to hone the knives using the right tools and just a little bit of your time.

When the knives on a planer/thicknesser are nice and sharp, the resulting surface on the wood only requires a light sanding before applying a finish.

How to sharpen

As I mentioned earlier, the job of a planer/ thicknesser is to prepare workpieces for your project. The milling operations of planing and thicknessing should result in a workpiece that's smooth and straight on both faces and edges and a consistent thickness and width. When the knives on the planer/ thicknesser start to become dull, you'll notice it in the surface quality of the wood.

Traditional cutterheads on planer/thicknessers are outfitted with two, three or more straight knives. High-speed steel (HSS) knives can be sharpened in the shop, and sometimes while installed on the machine. I will show you a couple of methods for sharpening the knives on a planer without removing them from the machine.

Some newer planer/thicknessers feature helical cutterheads with dozens of carbide cutters installed on them. These are an improvement over straight-knife cutterheads because they leave a much smoother surface on the wood. This is due to the shearing action of each knife edge as it approaches the wood. This angled attack on the wood fibres severs them cleanly for a smoother finish. Contrast this with straight planer/thicknesser knives where the entire length of the knife attacks the wood with each rotation. This can sometimes leave small ripples, or machining marks, in the wood that must be removed with a hand plane or by sanding.

Depending on the model of planer/thicknesser you have, you can buy a helical cutterhead to replace the original cutterhead. The cutters on helical cutterheads are replaceable, which also means they are disposable once they have become dull. These square cutters have four cutting edges. When one edge becomes dull, simply rotate the cutter to a fresh edge. When all four edges become dull, replace the cutter.

For the purposes of discussion in this chapter, I will focus on sharpening straight knives while installed on a planer. I will show you a commercial sharpening jig you can use. If you have easy access to the cutterhead on your thicknesser, you may be able to use the same tool to sharpen the knives.

The resulting surface left on the wood should be smooth and free of ridges. Dull or nicked knives will leave marks that must be sanded out.

A lot of newer portable or worktop thicknessers designed for home or hobbyist use much thinner, disposable knives. These should not be resharpened and most manufacturers don't recommend doing so. It's just as cost-effective and saves time to replace all of the knives at once when the old ones become dull.

Some vendors offer replacement high-speed steel (HSS) or carbide-tipped knives that fit some of these planers. These are often made of better steel that holds an edge longer.

Straight planer/thicknesser knives like these can often be sharpened. Some knives are disposable and should be replaced instead of resharpened.

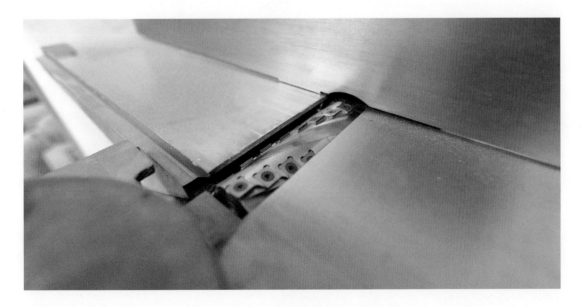

Helical cutterheads feature rows of square cutters. The spiral arrangement makes a smoother cut on the wood.

Sharpening planer knives

There are a couple of ways to sharpen your planer knives in place. Before you do so, take some time to clean the cutterhead with a stiff brush to remove caked-on sawdust.

The first method for sharpening is to use a commercial honing jig. This features an angled stone on one side and a square stone on the other. This allows you to dress both the back and the bevel of each planer knife.

The first thing to do is rotate the planer cutterhead for easy access to one of the knives.

You'll need to lock it in place with a wood wedge or shim to keep the cutterhead from rotating as you hone the knife.

Using the angled stone, as shown below, polish the bevel of the knife. You're looking for an even scratch pattern all the way across the length of the knife. The most critical point is at the cutting edge. This should be smooth all the way across.

With the cutterhead still locked in place, flip the honing jig over and use the square stone to touch up the back of the knife. Once that's done, unlock the

This honing jig can dress both the bevel and the back of the planer knife. Longer versions of this jig are available for thicknesser knives.

After the face of the bevel is dressed, use the square stone on the jig to touch up the back of the knife and remove any burrs that may have formed.

cutterhead to rotate it to the next knife and repeat the process.

Another method you can use to sharpen the planer knives while still installed in the cutterhead is to use a standard sharpening stone. To do this, you rub the stone across the bevel of the knife. Place a protective cover over the bed of the planer to protect it. I use a thin piece of plywood for this sharpening method.

Rotate the cutterhead so that the bevel on the knife is parallel to the bed of the planer. With the protective plywood in place on the infeed table, adjust the height of the table until the top of the plywood is flush with the knife's bevel. Lock the

cutterhead with a wedge or piece of wood to prevent it from rotating.

Now you can use a standard sharpening stone to dress the bevelled edge of the knife. You can progress through a series of grits to obtain a sharp edge.

With one knife sharpened, rotate the cutterhead to the next knife and repeat the process until all the knives are sharpened.

Maintaining an edge on planer/thicknesser knives is a simple process that can buy you time before you need to replace them.

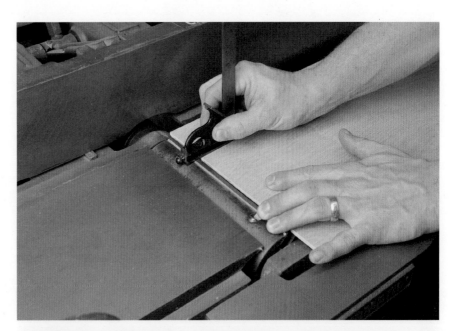

With a thin piece of plywood on the infeed table, lower the table until it is flush with the bevel on the planer knife.

With a sharpening stone placed flat on the plywood, move the stone back and forth across the bevel of the planer knife.

2:9
Drill bits

Step into almost any workshop and you're sure to find a box or drawer full of old drill bits. With a little patience and practice, some of those old drill bits can be brought back to life.

Sometimes it makes more sense to throw away a dull bit than to spend time sharpening it, especially for the smaller, less expensive, bits. We buy complete sets of drill bits because they cost less than buying the bits individually. Sometimes those sets consist of lower-quality bits that won't hold an edge for very long. The strategy I use in this case is to upgrade to a higher-quality bit as one wears out and becomes unusable. Replacing bits in the set one at a time like this upgrades your collection with better-quality bits.

If you wish to tackle sharpening your own drill bits, it's not difficult if you have the right tools and use proper techniques. I'll show you how to sharpen a few of the more common types of bits.

Twist drill bits are used for drilling metal (right). Spade bits are designed to quickly make larger holes (left). Brad-point bits are used for drilling clean holes in wood (centre).

Twist drill bits

Twist drill bits are the most common type of bits. They are readily available at any hardware store or home centre. They are designed to drill metal and other materials.

Twist bits are not the best for drilling wood, however, if you want the hole to have smooth edges without splintering. There are other bits that are better for drilling wood. I'll talk about those later.

If you look at the end of a twist drill bit, you'll see two or three cutting edges where the bit bites into the material you're drilling. The function of the flutes (spiral channels) is to pull chips out of the hole

Cutting edge

LEFT: *The cutting edges on a drill bit often become dull. Use a grinder to sharpen these edges.*

BELOW: *A split tip (left) offers two additional cutting edges to cut faster and reduce wear on the primary cutting edges versus a standard bit (right).*

as you advance the drill bit. As a twist bit begins to dull, the lip becomes rounded or deformed. You'll know the bit is dull when it takes a lot of effort to get the bit to engage the material. You may also see the tip of the drill bit getting hot and turning blue or black.

As I mentioned before, sharpness is defined as the intersection of two planes (see page 12). To sharpen the cutting lips of a drill bit, you need to grind away metal at the point. Those with a lot of experience can do this easily on a bench grinder.

When grinding drill bits, it is important to maintain the same tip angle around the circumference of the bit. Two common angles are 118° and 135°. The higher-angle bits are designed for cutting harder materials.

Even more importantly, the point of the bit must remain centred on the diameter of the bit.

This machine utilizes a chuck that holds a twist drill bit in the proper position during the sharpening process.

A diamond-coated wheel inside the unit grinds the tip of the drill bit at the proper angle as you rotate the chuck in the sharpening port.

Otherwise, the bit will 'walk' across the material when drilling instead of cutting into it at a defined point. Some bits, especially those with a 135°-angled tip, feature a 'split point'. You can see the difference between a standard point and split-point bit in the photos at the bottom of page 132.

Experienced machinists have learned how to quickly sharpen a twist drill bit by hand using a bench grinder. Because of the considerations I mentioned above, those of us with less experience are better off using a grinding jig or drill-sharpening machine.

A mechanized drill bit sharpener is great for restoring twist drill bits. Versions are available for the home hobbyist that won't break the bank. If you wear out a lot of drill bits, this is a great option.

These machines work so well because they are designed to maintain a consistent angle as the drill bit is sharpened. It takes the guesswork and frustration out of sharpening drill bits.

Most machines accommodate different point angles on twist drill bits by adjusting the bit's angle of attack against the sharpening abrasive. This

You can sharpen any twist bit in just a few seconds. A drill bit can be sharpened many times before it needs to be replaced.

makes the machine more versatile and able to sharpen a much wider range of bits.

A mechanized sharpener is a great tool for maintaining your collection of drill bits. You can restore those old bits you've been throwing in a box because you couldn't bear to throw them away. These machines take the fear and fuss out of sharpening drill bits.

A note about brad-point bits: brad-point bits are a form of twist bit that have been specially ground for drilling in wood. They feature two outside cutting spurs that leave a clean hole. The small centre point helps keep the bit from wandering off-centre. Because of the special shape of the tips of these bits, they can be difficult to sharpen without specialized equipment. As with standard drill bits, I replace the dull bits in my set with new ones as they become dull.

Brad-point bits have a special geometry designed for drilling in wood. This makes them difficult to sharpen.

Spade (paddle) bits

Spade bits get their name from their flat shape, which resembles a garden spade or a paddle. They are among some of the least expensive bits available. For this reason, there can be times when it makes sense to purchase a replacement bit instead of trying to sharpen it. For example, if the shaft has become bent, it's a throwaway. If the cutting edges are severely dinged or showing signs of burning, it may be time to replace it. If, however, it's simply not cutting as it should and hasn't been abused, sharpening the bit is a viable option that will save you the cost of a new bit.

Spade bits, despite their simple design, are amazingly effective at drilling larger holes in wood.

Tip

When you are using a spade bit to drill a hole through the material and you want a clean exit hole without splintering and tearout, drill from one side of the workpiece until the centre point just starts to poke through the back side. Then drill from the back side, making sure the centre point engages the small centre hole. Drill through the workpiece. You should be left with a hole with clean edges on both sides of the material.

A spade bit has a sharp centre point that quickly engages the wood and keeps the bit from wandering as you drill. These long points will generally have sharp cutting edges along their length. Some bits have a screw thread that helps draw the bit into the wood as you drill.

Two outside spurs score the edge of the hole, which leaves a clean cut without splintering and tearout. Finally, the flat, bevelled areas between the spur and centre point act like a chisel or hand plane to shave the wood to create the hole.

Spade bits are ground at the factory with grinding wheels on specialized machinery to form the cutting edges. To maintain those edges in the home workshop, a small tapered diamond file can be useful. To touch up a dull spade bit, there are six areas where you can focus your attention. The first are the two bevelled cutting edges.

Carefully angle the file so that it rests flat on the bevelled cutting edge. File the bevel until it is smooth.

Use a small file to clean up the inside face of each spur. You'll want to create a sharp edge to cleanly slice the wood fibres at the circumference of the hole.

After the bevel on one cutting edge is touched up, flip the bit over to address the other edge. Be careful to ensure that the file doesn't cut into the spurs or centre point.

Touching up the two outside spurs is next. Just make sure you file the inside face of each spur. If you file the outer edge, you'll change the diameter and cutting geometry of the bit, which can make it perform poorly when drilling.

The last thing to do is make sure the pair of cutting edges of the centre point are nice and sharp. This just takes a few strokes on each side with the file, following the original bevel angle.

That's it. Sharpening a dull spade bit is easy and takes almost no time.

A few swipes with the file along the cutting edges of the centre point should be all you need to create sharp edges.

Tip

Some spade bits have a small hole drilled through the face. This style of bit is often used by electricians to drill through wood framing in a building to run electrical wiring. Once the electrician drills through the wood, they can fasten an electrical wire to the hole in the bit and pull the wire back through the hole.

Forstner-style drill bits

Forstner drill bits are named after their inventor, Benjamin Forstner. This is a unique style of drill bit many variations of which have been made since 1886.

A Forstner bit excels at drilling flat-bottomed holes in wood. The centre point is barely long enough to engage the wood before the outside cutting edge scores the circumference of the hole.

There are many variations of Forstner bits available. The common features among them all are the centre point and flat cutting edges (similar to spade bits opposite). The outside diameter of the bit, however, can vary greatly in its configuration.

Simpler Forstner bits feature a pair of cutting edges, or teeth, on the outside rim of the bit (see page 140). The entire rim has been sharpened with a bevel on the inside. This helps score the wood fibres as it drills for clean, professional results.

Other Forstner styles are manufactured with a series of teeth around the outside rim of the bit, as in the right bit on page 140. These resemble saw teeth.

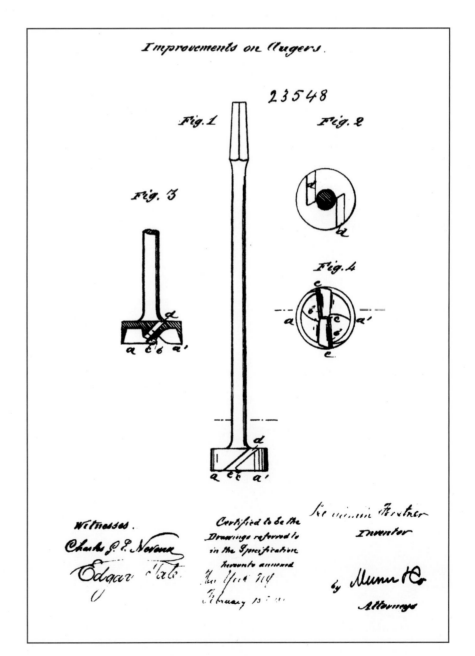

As this original 1886 patent drawing shows, the Forstner drill bit was a revolution in drilling technology at the time.

They can be more effective at cutting through tough woods and keep the bit cooler as it drills.

As with a spade bit, sharpening a Forstner bit involves addressing all of the cutting edges. For this, the small, tapered diamond file comes in handy. I start by touching up the flat cutting edges on the inside.

Next, you can turn your attention to the outer rim. For a Forstner bit with a sawtooth configuration, use the small file to clean up the cutting edges of each tooth.

For a traditional-style Forstner bit with a continuous rim, I like to use a rotary tool with a cone-shaped grinding stone. With the bit clamped lightly in a vice to avoid damaging the shaft, carefully use the grinder to polish the inside bevel all the way around.

The last area to address is the flat face on the back side of the bevelled cutters. These lift the chips out of the hole as you're drilling. You don't need to go overboard here. I just like to make sure there are no burrs at the cutting edge.

Learning how to sharpen drill bits is a skill that can save you money and time in the workshop. All it takes is a little patience, practice and persistence.

Forstner bits come in a variety of styles, but they all drill larger holes with flat bottoms.

Maintaining the same bevel angle, file the bevelled cutting edges smooth.

A small file is the perfect tool for sharpening each tooth on the outside rim of this style of Forstner bit.

Use a rotary tool with a conical grindstone to polish the inside bevel around the rim of a Forstner bit.

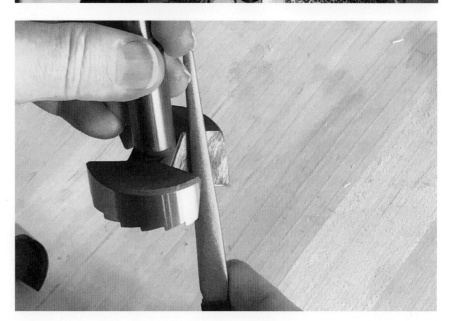

Make sure there are no burrs along the cutting edges by making a few strokes with the file flat on the face behind the bevel.

About the author

Randall Maxey has been woodworking for most of his life. He has contributed to two other woodworking books by GMC Publications: *Outdoor Woodworking Games: 20 Fun Projects to Make* and *Woodworking Basics: The Principles and Skills of Good Joinery*. He is a contributing editor to *Furniture & Cabinetmaking*, *Woodsmith* and *WOOD* magazines. He also teaches part-time at the Florida School of Woodwork.

Randall owns a custom woodworking business, Cherry Ridge Woodworks. He is the founder of MiniMaxWorkshop.com, which supports the idea that you can build great projects in limited spaces. He resides with his wife in Florida.

Acknowledgements

I think some people have the mistaken notion that writing a book is a simple affair. Just sit down, put words on pages and submit it for publication. Nothing could be further from the truth. Authoring a book is an intense time commitment that involves a lot of people. This book would not have been possible without the support and guidance of several individuals.

A few years ago, Alan Goodsell drafted me to help him co-author two books by GMC Publications. Alan is a joy to work with and has become a dear friend. Without his encouragement and knowledge, this book would not have become a reality.

There are many folks at GMC Publications who have been instrumental in pushing this book along, so thanks go to Jonathan Phillips, Jonathan Bailey, Dominique Page, Wendy McAngus and Emma Foster. There are many others behind the scenes who made this book a reality.

Then there is my wife, Sheryl. She has served as my chief supporter, proofreader and photo assistant. Thank you, dear, for allowing your living room to become a photo studio and warehouse. Without your love and emotional support, I would have floundered long ago.

Thanks to Andrew Gibson for taking the time to shoot a few photographs for me. You are a dear friend. Thanks for jumping in at a moment's notice.

Many photos were shot at the Florida School of Woodwork, where I also teach part-time. Thanks to Kate Swann for allowing me to invade her space for a short time during the writing of this book.

Scott and Vanessa Leonard have earned my appreciation for allowing me to shoot photos in their gorgeous kitchen.

John Carmona has offered me a wealth of knowledge and technical expertise. Thanks, John, for answering all of my questions, your patience and your valuable comments on the text of the book.

There are many others – too numerous to mention individually – who deserve my gratitude.

The following companies have provided much-needed technical and product support:

Darex Drill Doctor
Darex.com

DMT
dmtsharp.com

Lee Valley Tools
leevalley.com

M-Power Tools
m-powertools.com

Rikon Power Tools
Rikontools.com

Rockler
rockler.com

SharpeningSupplies.com

Smith's Products
smithproducts.com

Trend
Trend-usa.com
Trend-uk.com

Wixey
wixey.com

Woodcraft
woodcraft.com

Work Sharp
worksharptools.com

Picture Credits

All photographs by Randall Maxey, apart from p129: Andrew Gibson; p132 (bottom): Darex, LLC. Images from Shutterstock.com: Olef (p2, p64); Pandit Chanthong (p10); ezolyzm (p14); T photography (p18); LegART (p20); Edinaldo Maciel (p26); Geartooth Productions (p46); ezolyzm (p48); MarjanCermelj (p82); Tomy Hovington (p84 top); Piyachok Thawornmat (p88); luri (p90); Natasha Breen (p98); NDanko (p104); sevenke (p106); VDB Photos (p107 top); brillenstimmer (p107 bottom left); BMJ (p107 bottom right); mihalec (p120); New Africa (p124); Sergey Borisov_88 (p126); Oleksandr Kostiuchenko (p127 T); C5 Media (p127 B); Mark Anthony Ray (p130) and Piotr Wytrazek (p135).

Index

First published 2020 by Guild of Master Craftsman Publications Ltd,
Castle Place, 166 High Street, Lewes, East Sussex, BN7 1XU, UK.

Text © Randall A. Maxey, 2020
Copyright in the Work © GMC Publications Ltd, 2020

ISBN 978 1 78494 440 7

PUBLISHER: Jonathan Bailey
PRODUCTION: Jim Bulley and Jo Pallett
SENIOR PROJECT EDITOR: Wendy McAngus
MANAGING ART EDITOR: Gilda Pacitti
EDITOR: Nicola Hodgson
DESIGN: Ginny Zeal
PHOTOGRAPHERS: Randall A. Maxey, Andrew Gibson

Colour origination by GMC Reprographics
Printed and bound in China

To order a book, or to request a catalogue, contact:
GMC Publications Ltd
Castle Place, 166 High Street,
Lewes, East Sussex,
BN7 1XU
United Kingdom
Tel: +44 (0)1273 488005
www.gmcbooks.com